Philip Francis

Two Speeches in the House of Commons

On the Original East-India Bill and on the Amended Bill, on the 16th and

26th of July, 1784

Philip Francis

Two Speeches in the House of Commons
On the Original East-India Bill and on the Amended Bill, on the 16th and 26th of July, 1784

ISBN/EAN: 9783337059194

Printed in Europe, USA, Canada, Australia, Japan

Cover: Foto ©Suzi / pixelio.de

More available books at **www.hansebooks.com**

TWO SPEECHES

IN THE

HOUSE of COMMONS

ON

THE ORIGINAL EAST-INDIA BILL

AND ON

THE AMENDED BILL,

ON

THE 16th AND 26th OF JULY, 1784,

BY

PHILIP FRANCIS, Esq.

LONDON:

Printed for J. DEBRETT, opposite Burlington House, Piccadilly.

M,DCC,LXXXIV.

HOUSE OF COMMONS.

FRIDAY, JULY 16, 1784.

" THE order of the day being read, for the
" Houfe to refolve itfelf into a Committee of
" the whole Houfe, upon the Bill for the better
" regulation and management of the affairs of the
" Eaft-India Company, and of the Britifh pof-
" feffions in India, and for eftablifhing a Court of
" Judicature for the more fpeedy and effectual
" trial of perfons accufed of offences committed
" in the Eaft Indies; the Speaker put the queftion,
" *That he fhould now leave the chair?*"

Mr. FRANCIS.

Mr. SPEAKER,

I am forry that I muft be obliged to oppofe
your leaving the chair. My opinion of the bill
will not allow me to confent to its going to a
Committee; for I not only think it materially de-

fective

fective in the detail, but liable to fundamental
and effential objections. Particular provifions might
be added, improved, or omitted; but objections,
that go to the foundation and effence of the bill,
are not to be removed by any alterations, that would
not make it compleatly a new one. I have atten-
tively confidered the fubject; and I mean, if the
Houfe will permit me, to fubmit to you my opinion
of it, more at large than I fhould venture to do
any other. I mean to examine the principles as
well as the provifions of the bill; — a tafk, I fear,
not to be performed without a long and a tedious
difcuffion. To *me* the tafk is particularly heavy,
but I am bound to undertake it by many obliga-
tions. The labour we are engaged in does not
offer *me* the fame hopes, which it may have fug-
gefted to others : I am not encouraged to engage
in it by a fanguine expectation of fuccefs. I very
much fear, that the object of our prefent deliberation is dead. You have neglected it too long.
You have fuffered it to fall into a ftate of ruin from
which, I fear, no remedy within the reach of human
wifdom can recover it. But a great authority, under which I had the honour and good fortune to be
bred, has taught me, *that duty may furvive hope.*
— On this principle alone, I am ftill ready to take
my fhare in the duty, though I cannot partake in
any hope of its fuccefs.

The views and principles of the bill may naturally and properly be divided into three diftinct general heads. — Firft, the new arrangement and diftribution

tribution of power at home, with all its probable effects and influence on our domeſtic government.— On this part of the ſubject I ſhall confine myſelf ſtrictly to the fact, which I think will be eaſily eſtabliſhed, that there is a compleat and abſolute transfer of the whole power and patronage of the Eaſt-India Company into the hands of the Crown. Of the effects of this transfer of power, of its probable influence on our own Government, and of the danger with which it may threaten the Conſtitution of England, I do not mean to offer an opinion. If thoſe topics have not already been ſufficiently diſcuſſed, they properly belong to the department, and ſhould be reſerved for the employment of the greateſt abilities in this country. A right honourable gentleman near me will do juſtice to the ſubject.

The ſecond diviſion of the bill includes the arrangements and regulations intended for the Governments abroad; and on this I ſhall hope to be permitted to enlarge. Without pretending to ſuperior qualifications, or preſuming to dictate to the wiſdom of the Houſe, I am perſuaded you will liſten to information, which only profeſſes to be derived from experience.

The third diviſion regards the new plan of criminal judicature propoſed to be introduced into England, for trying offences committed in India. On this laſt point my opinion will not be delivered in many words, but the words that I make uſe of ſhall be the ſtrongeſt I can find.

Sir,

Sir, There are two preliminary obfervations, which arife on a general view of the bill, and which I wifh the Houfe to carry along with them, through the difcuffion of all the parts of it. Firft, that the whole bill on the face of it is remedial; that it is a remedy of a new and violent nature, neceffary perhaps, but neceffary only on the fuppofition of fome great and inveterate diforders, both at home and abroad, which, though conftantly implied, are no where ftated.

Secondly, Sir, admitting fuch diforders to exift, I think it will appear, through the whole plan of the bill, that the remedy applied is in every inftance directly the reverfe of what the diforder requires. With refpect to the Governments abroad, the ac-knowledged grievance is, that the powers, hitherto intrufted, have been groffly and notorioufly abufed. But you will find that, in the contemplation of this bill, the true and natural remedy for an abufe of power is to increafe it. With refpect to the Com-pany's Government at home, the conftant complaint of the Directors has been, that their power over their fervants was too feeble to enforce obedience, that their authority was difregarded, and their orders avowedly and conftantly difobeyed. You have facts in abundance, reported to you by your Committees, to fatisfy the Houfe that thefe complaints of the Directors are perfectly well founded. Now, Sir, in the contemplation of this bill, the remedy for difobedience of orders is to ftrengthen the power that difobeys; and when infulted authority calls for

fupport,

fupport, either, in effect to reduce it to nothing, or, what is ftill worfe, to fuffer it to exift and to make it contemptible. The pretended power, left in the hands of the Directors, is a mockery of the degraded ftate of thofe unfortunate gentlemen. It is worfe than ufelefs; for fince, in fact, they are only to be the channel of the operations of a fuperior power, you diminifh even that power, which un-queftionably the bill propofes to eftablifh, and ex-pofe it to fhare in the contempt attached to the medium, through which it is to act. In thefe ob-fervations I mean only to ftate the general refult and impreffion of the bill, without immediately re-ferring to the fpecific evidence, from which they are deduced. The fhorteft and cleareft way to eftablifh the truth of them is to enter at once into the detail of the bill, and to follow it as it goes.

Sir, the very outfet of the bill is effentially de-fective. When an act of legiflative power is applied to the total alteration of an exifting Government, it muft of neceffity be fuppofed that fuch Govern-ment is either radically corrupt, or unfaithfully ad-miniftered. No man, I prefume, will difpute that fuch is the fact in the general government of the Eaft-India Company's affairs. The prefent bill, through every part of it, fuppofes what it no where avows, that nothing lefs than a vigorous interpofition of the Legiflature can fave the object. For aught that appears in the preamble of this act, where the general grounds of it fhould naturally be fet forth, the territorial poffeffions, for whofe *better* govern-

ment

ment we are going to provide, may be perfectly well governed at prefent. For want of this effential preliminary, the whole body of the bill is in effect a conclufion without premifes, a remedy without a difeafe, a penalty without a crime. The omiffion of fuch a preamble to fuch a bill as this will appear extraordinary as well as improper, to thofe who recollect with how much force and energy the Chancellor of the Exchequer, in opening the plan and principles of the bill, infifted on the magnitude of thofe crimes and abufes, which demanded and juftified a proportionate effort of power to punifh or correct them. He was not very referved in his defcription of the offenders, or of their offences, but painted them both in the blackeft colours. It is much to be regretted, that the fubftance, at leaft, of his opinion of Indian delinquency fhould be no where recorded for the benefit of his friends.

The new Board of Commiffioners for the affairs of India is to confift of certain Members of His Majefty's Privy Council, and they are to be invefted with the fuperintendence and control over all the Britifh territorial poffeffions in the Eaft Indies, *and over the affairs of the United Company of Merchants trading thereto.* The powers, conveyed by the latter part of this claufe, evidently and expreffly include the Company's commerce. The affairs of a Company of Merchants trading to India can only be commercial. Let the Court of Directors look to it. I am perfectly aware, that in a fubfequent claufe it is provided, that if the Commiffioners fend any orders

ders

ders to the Court of Directors, which, in their opinion, shall relate to points not connected with the
territorial government or revenues, they may apply
to the King in Council for redress; that is, if
they are dissatisfied with the judgement of His Majesty's Ministers at one Board, they may appeal to
His Majesty's Ministers at another. The power
given is unlimited. The appeal against the exercise of it is nugatory.

The Court of Directors are to be governed and
bound by the orders they receive from the Commissioners; and are not to send dispatches of any
kind to India, without their previous approbation.

The Commissioners may send their own orders
originally to the Directors, who are obliged to in-
sert such orders in their dispatches, pursuant to the
tenor thereof; that is, in the same words.

If the Commissioners should be of opinion that
the case requires secrecy, they may send their own
orders directly to the Governments in India, without any communication with the Court of Directors,
who are not to be trusted even with the knowledge
of measures, in which the most essential interests,
the safety, and, perhaps, the existence of the India
Company may be involved. In the same clause,
the Commissioners may not only send their orders to
the Governments abroad without the knowledge of
the Directors, but, what is much more extraordinary, and much more alarming, they may send se-
cret instructions to the Commanders in Chief in India, independent of the Civil Government on the
spot.

ſpot. If there be no miſtake in the conſtruction of this-clauſe; if it be ſeriouſly intended to give this power to the Miniſters of the Crown, there is no clauſe in the bill that more urgently demands the attention of the Houſe. By another clauſe, the nomination and appointment of all the Commanders in Chief in India, and of perſons to ſucceed to the command in caſe of vacancy, are directly veſted in the Crown; and theſe officers are required to obey whatever orders they receive from the King's Miniſters, not only independent of the Directors at home, but of the Civil Government of the Preſidency to which they belong. I ſtate the facts as I find them, and ſhall leave them without comment to the judgement of the Houſe.

The general patronage of the Company is profeſſedly left with the Court of Directors, but with exceptions and reſtrictions which really reduce it to nothing. The Commanders in Chief and their immediate ſucceſſors, at all the Preſidencies, are to be under the immediate appointment of the Crown. By this proviſion the military is ſeparated from the civil power of the Company's government. The Court of Directors, who pay the army, and whoſe general authority over it is apparently continued, can neither appoint, nor remove the perſons who command it.

With reſpect to the offices of Governor General, Preſidents, and Members of the ſeveral Councils in India, the Directors, it is true, may nominate and appoint: but it deſerves to be conſidered, that they

who

who appoint are not permitted to remove; that power is exclusively vested in the Crown; and even the pretended power of appointing to these offices is ineffectual. Their nomination is to be subject to his Majesty's approbation. If the King disapproves, the Directors must proceed to another nomination; and so on, *toties quoties*, until persons shall be appointed *who shall be approved by His Majesty*. This is the way, in which the patronage of all the principal offices in India is disposed of. All other promotions, civil and military, are to be made according to seniority of appointment in a regular progressive succession; and the Directors are prohibited from sending out any new servants, civil or military, until certain establishments shall be completed, and then, only to fill up the vacancies that may happen therein. I do not mean to blame these last regulations: but, if all the preceding exceptions and limitations are combined, it is evident, that no real patronage will be left with the Directors, or, at the utmost, a patronage to operate upon trifles. Not so the powers given to the Commissioners. In every department of the Company's affairs, *their* direct authority, or their indirect influence, is real and effective. On the real principles of this bill, whether acknowledged or not, the Court of Directors ought to be abolished. To leave a shadow of power after the substance of it is gone, is to establish a contradiction, which can only do mischief. Whenever the constitution of any government is essentially altered, the forms should not be allowed to survive

C the

the essence. Under the shelter of these forms, things will be done, or duties will be neglected, for which no man will be responsible. No despotism was ever so severe as that, which existed in the form of a republic. In whatever degree the powers reserved to the Directors are effective, they can only be productive of mischievous effects. They can only clash with, and retard the operations of the superior Board, and furnish them both with pretences for accusing each other of whatever may happen amiss.

Now, Sir, I submit it to the House, to determine whether my first proposition be not sufficiently established, that in every sense in which power can be suspicious, in which power can be mischievous to the thing subject to it, or dangerous to objects not immediately connected with it, there is by this bill a complete and absolute transfer of power from the India Company to the Crown. *I* consider it only as it affects the Government of India, and shall pursue the remaining clauses in the order in which they stand.

I have already taken the liberty of observing to the Chancellor of the Exchequer, that the bill makes no provision for the situation of a Commander in Chief of all the Company's forces in India. The office exists, though it be not actually filled up, and it ought to be provided for. That officer has always had a seat in the Supreme Council; of course, there must be a mistake in the seventeenth clause, which gives voice and precedence in Council

fo the Commander in Chief of the Prefidency of
Fort William, as if he had a feat there, which, in
fact, he never had. The miftake muft be corrected.

From the terms of the nineteenth claufe, I conclude that Lord Macartney is to be removed from
the Government of Fort St. George ; that is, that
he is to be facrificed to the views and refentments
of the Government of Bengal. I have not the honour of knowing Lord Macartney, nor have I a
connection with him of any kind : but, in order to
be convinced that the noble Lord has done his duty,
it is fufficient for me to know who the perfons are,
and what the combination is, that are united againft
him. By a different courfe of conduct, *their* enmity
is not to be incurred. The moment I knew the
fact, I drew the conclufion — I forefaw the confe-
quence, and foretold it to his friends : *This man is
doing his duty, and affuredly he'll be recalled for it.*
Comparing this claufe with another that relates to
Fort William, the Houfe will obferve, that in Bengal, which is the feat of power, and where, if mif-
chief has been done in India, the fource of it muft
exift, there is to be no change of hands ; but, in the
fubordinate fettlements, there is to be an univerfal
fweep.

The wifdom and neceffity of the thirtieth claufe,
by which the General Court of Proprietors are re-
ftrained from interfering with *any act, order, refolution, matter, or proceeding of the Court of Directors,*
will, in this Houfe at leaft, be generally acknow-

ledged.

ledged. All parties, I believe, are agreed on the neceffity of putting an end to the cabals of that affembly. Every bill, from every quarter, that has hitherto been propofed for the better regulation of the Company's affairs, makes fpecial provifion for this favourite object. I therefore give the claufe my entire and hearty approbation. At the fame time, Sir, I cannot help obferving, that the principle and object of this provifion is not to be reconciled to the language, or rather to the cry, by which a bill that paffed the Houfe of Commons laft year was run down, and the honourable perfon who moved it, for a moment difpoffeffed of his popularity, and driven from his ftation. If the rights conveyed by an exclufive charter be in their nature *facred,* they can no more be invaded in part, than they can be wholly refumed. If the charter itfelf be *facred,* it ought to be *inviolable*; or, if any part of it be more effentially *facred* than the reft, it muft be that, which fecures to the Proprietors the control and direction of their own affairs. In this refpect, the prefent bill adopts the very fame principle, by which a much better was defeated. It affumes a difcretion, where, on the profeffed principles of thofe who defend it, there fhould be none. It takes or leaves juft as much of the Company's charter, as fuits the purpofes of the prefent Adminiftration.

The object of the thirty-fecond claufe is proper. The fubordinate Prefidencies fhould either be dependent on the fuperintendence and control of the
Go-

Governor General and Council in *all* cafes, or totally exempt from it. We know by experience, that an attempt to fubject them to a *partial* control is not likely to fucceed. We know that it has hitherto produced no good effect. On the other hand, it is evidently abfurd and hazardous, that the members of one ftate, and the parts of one fyftem, fhould not be united under one power, whenever they are to act, and not move together under a fingle direction. There is no alternative, therefore, but to eftablifh a general authority at Fort William, and to infift on a general fubmiffion to it : but, at the fame time, let care be taken to unite the powers, and ftrengthen the authority at home in the fame proportion.

The thirty-third claufe is fo very incorrect and obfcure, that, I confefs, I fhould be glad to fee it tranflated into common fenfe. It is faid, that the rules, ordinances, and regulations, which the Governor General and Council are empowered to iffue, fhall extend to all rules, ordinances, and regulations made by the faid Governor General and Council. If this be not pofitively nonfenfe, it is, at leaft, an extraordinary way of removing all former *queftions and doubts* upon the fubject. Whoever drew up the claufe evidently knew nothing of the matter. So far from explaining the queftions, or removing the doubts to which he alludes, he does not even know what they were, nor what they referred to. The only queftion that ever arofe in Bengal, concerning the power granted by the act of 1773 to the
Governor

Governor General and Council, to make rules and ordinances for the settlement of Fort William, was, to what *things*, to what *subject matter*, and not to what persons or places, the power extended; and this, indeed, is a doubt which it would be proper to clear up. If it be intended to give a general legislative power, the terms you make use of must be much more comprehensive and much more explicit.

The thirty-seventh clause declares, that *to pursue schemes of conquest, and extension of dominion in India, are measures repugnant to the wish, the honour, and policy of this nation.* Sir, I wish to see a proposition so full of truth and wisdom, not only acknowledged, but enforced. In this most essential view, the plan of the bill is most essentially defective. It alludes to facts and offences which are not stated, and to criminals whom, so far from attempting to punish, it does not even venture to describe. If such facts and criminals do not exist, the whole bill is a superfluity built upon a falsehood. It supposes imaginary disorders, for the imaginary merit of correcting them. But if they really exist, it is in vain to expect that they will be checked or prevented by the empty threats of a Legislature, that contents itself with piling up laws upon laws, and regulations on regulations — of a Legislature, that never has hitherto been obeyed, yet always looks forward to future obedience. Reward and punishment are the right and left hand of Government. It is the office of the head to frame and denounce the law, but it is the hand that must enforce it. In another point
of

of view, the bill is unjuſt as well as impotent. It makes no diſtinction between thoſe perſons, who have uniformly acted on the principles you approve, and others, who have uniformly acted on the principles you condemn. In not ſtating *any* to be innocent, it ſuppoſes *all* to be guilty. Now, Sir, I ſhall do what the mover of the bill has not had courage to do. I attach reſponſibility to power, and I affirm, that, at the end of the year 1777, the whole political power of the Britiſh empire in India, nominally veſted in the Governor General and Council, was really and ſubſtantially veſted in Mr. Haſtings. If Mr. Haſtings, ſupported by one Member of the Supreme Council againſt the other two, be not excluſively reſponſible for the war which was undertaken at that period, for the *avowed* purpoſe of conqueſt and extenſion of dominion, which carried deſolation with it wherever it extended, and which has ended in the ruin of the Eaſt-India Company, it is fit that Parliament and the nation ſhould know, nay, it is the duty of Parliament to inquire, who was the author of the war, and who is to be anſwerable for it. Facts, it will be ſaid, may be very differently repreſented, and variouſly accounted for, eſpecially at ſo great a diſtance as from India to England. Sir, I well know the facility, with which facts at ſuch a diſtance may be ſtated to advantage. But principles formally declared, and deliberately avowed, are not to be diſguiſed or retracted. They ſtand for public judgement, and they demand it. If the Houſe have any doubt about the fact, let them look to the acknowledged

ledged principles of the perfon, to whom the fact is imputed. Does Mr. Haftings himfelf deny, that conqueft and extent of dominion were his object in the purfuit of the Maratta war ? No, Sir ; he avows it. Let him anfwer for himfelf. I will not run the rifque of doing him an injuftice.

" If the Britifh arms and influence have fuffered
" a fevere check in the Weftern world, it is the
" more incumbent on thofe who are charged with
" the interefts of Great Britain in the Eaft, to exert
" themfelves for the retrieval of the national lofs ;
" that we have the means in our power ; and that,
" with fuch fuperior advantages as we poffefs over
" every power which can oppofe us, *we fhould not*
" *act merely on the defenfive*.*"

In thefe explicit words you have all the policy and all the juftice of the Maratta war : *If we have fuffered loffes in the Weft, let us repair them in the Eaft ; wherever we are powerful, it is our bufinefs to attack.* Surely, Sir, if no other evidence exifted, it would not be very unreafonable to prefume, that Mr. Haftings's meafures have been formed on the principles he profeffes.

I am ready to admit that the claufe in queftion does all that can be done, by mere legiflative prohibition, to put a ftop to fuch meafures in future. Yet I very much fear that the general rule will be defeated by the exception that attends it. The Governor General and Council are not to make war, or to commence hoftilities againft any of the coun-

* Confultation of 22d June, 1778.

try powers, *unless such powers shall be actually making preparations for the commencement of hostilities* against us or our allies. I beg leave to assure the House, that whenever the Governor General and Council are disposed to make war upon their neighbours, they can at all times fabricate a case to suit their purpose, and send home a mass of incontrovertible evidence to support it. — The exception in the next clause, by which a similar latitude is given to Fort St. George and Bombay, is not so dangerous, because those Presidencies are nearer to a power that may control them. They cannot make war, if the Governor General and Council be seriously determined against it. But again I tell you, that one example is worth a hundred laws.

I am not very conversant with the affairs of the coast of Coromandel, and therefore shall offer but a single observation on the several clauses that relate to the liquidation of the debts due to British subjects from the Nabob of Arcot, the Rajah of Tanjore, and any other of the native protected princes in India. The labour of inquiring into and liquidating these debts, which the bill imposes on the Governor General and Council, in addition to their own immediate duties, will be very heavy, and, I believe, equally useless. They may adjust the account; but I have no conception how the debts are to be paid out of an exhausted revenue, and a ruined country. I believe it to be impossible, unless a preference is to be given to the private debts before

D   those

thofe of the Company, which, I prefume, is not intended.

The final fettlement of the prefent indeterminate rights and poffeffions of the Nabob of Arcot and the Rajah of Tanjore, with refpect to each other, is a juft, a neceffary, and an attainable object. The principles, on which the fettlement is to be made, appear to me to be the beft that could be adopted. But I moft ftrongly object to, and proteft againft the idea of leaving the execution of the meafure to the Governor General and Council. The power, which predominates in that Government, is notorioufly partial to the Nabob of Arcot, and hoftile to the Rajah of Tanjore. The tribunal, to which you refer the parties, is prejudiced in favour of the ftronger of the two, and, if its intentions were ever fo upright, fhould not be trufted with the power of judging between them. Neither is it neceffary. There is no queftion of right between the contending parties, which may not be decided as properly and as effectually in England as it can be in Bengal. The Court of Directors have all the materials before them: they may determine the points in difpute, and fend their orders directly to the Prefident and Council of Fort St. George, to carry their decifion into effect. If they *can* do it, they *ought* to do it.

On a fimilar principle of reafon and juftice, I object to the mode adopted in the next claufe, for the profeffed purpofe of reinftating certain Rajahs, Zemindars, Polygars, and other landholders, who have

have been difpoffeffed of their lands. The claims
of the parties are to be referred to the refpective
Prefidencies, who are *to inquire into, and determine
upon them :* that is, if injuftice has been done, the
perfons, who have done it, are to repair it at their
difcretion. Is there any colour of propriety, is
there any prudence in fuch a delegation of power ?
or do you think it would be effectual ? For example, do you believe that any orders from the Court
of Directors, or even from the higheft power in
this country, could engage Mr. Haftings to liften
to the claims of the Rajah of Benares ? Can he be
reafonably deemed an impartial judge of fuch
claims ? He has told the Directors*, that " if
" they fhould proceed to order the reftoration of
" Rajah Cheyt Sing, *and, if the Council fhould re-
" folve to execute the order,* he would inftantly give
" up his ftation and the fervice." He fuppofes it
will be a queftion in the Council, whether the order
of the Directors fhall be executed or not ; and he
fairly apprifes them of his own refolution to oppofe
it. For my own part, I am perfuaded that he would
hazard his life rather than fubmit to carry the order
into execution himfelf. Yet, if ever there was a
cafe that called upon the national honour and huma-
nity for juftice and protection, affuredly it is that of
the Rajah of Benares.

The next claufe is material indeed. The well-
being, if not the exiftence of the natives of all

* 20th March, 1783.

your

your Eaſtern Dominions, depends on a firm eſtabliſh-
ment of that principle of taxation, which appears to
be the objeét of the clauſe. Ever ſince I have
known any thing of the ſubjeét, or had an opportunity of offering an opinion about it, it has been
the labour and effort of my life to inculcate and
eſtabliſh the truth of this propoſition — *that the. tribute, rent, ſervice, or payment to be paid by the ſeveral
landbolders, of whatever denomination, ſhould be fixed
and unalterable.* The profeſſed objeét of this clauſe
is the real objeét, and reſult of every concluſion, that
my underſtanding is capable of deducing from experience and refleétion. The means, taken to accom-
pliſh it, are the very worſt that could be thought of.
After twenty years poſſeſſion of the Dewanny, after
twenty years colleétion of the revenues, the fixation
of the rents is ſtill to be a queſtion for future inveſ-
tigation. — Good God! Sir, are theſe inquiſitions
into the property of our Indian ſubjeéts — are theſe
ſcrutinies into the value of their eſtates *never* to
have an end! Are the natives of India *never* to have
a quietus under an Engliſh Government! — In the
year 1784 you order the Governments abroad to *de-
viſe ſuch methods as ſhall to them ſeem moſt fitting and
convenient to eſtabliſh a fixed and unalterable tribute!*
The language held by the Direétors, ſeven years
ago, on a ſimilar occaſion, is wiſer and more hu-
mane than yours, and ought to be a leſſon to you.
In July, 1777, ſpeaking of a new mode of inquiſi-
tion propoſed and eſtabliſhed by Mr. Haſtings, they
ſaid, " In the preſent ſtate of the buſineſs, our ſur-
" priſe

" prife and concern were great on finding, by our
" Governor General's minute of the firft of No-
" vember, 1776, that, after more than feven years
" inveftigation, information is ftill fo incomplete,
" as to render another innovation, ftill more extra-
" ordinary than any of the former, abfolutely ne-
" ceffary to the formation of a new fettlement."

But the prefent courfe, it feems, is taken, *in order to prevent any corrupt or oppreffive practices.* —
Sir, the Court of Directors are in poffeffion of annual accounts of the revenues of Bengal fince the
year 1766. They have an account before them of
the demand, receipt, and balance of every refpective year. In fhort, Sir, they poffefs every poffible
light and information on the fubject, which the
Government of Bengal ought to look for, or would
be able to obtain. They may take the collections
of any one year for a ftandard, or, what is much
better, they may take an average of the collections
of feveral years, and determine at once, and for
ever, what all the principal diftricts fhall invariably
pay. Perhaps it may be neceffary, though I do not
think it will, to leave fome parts of the minuter
diftribution to the power upon the fpot. The lefs
you leave to it the better. The only danger of the
mode I propofe, or of any mode of fixation that
can be propofed, is this — that, take what period or
what average you will, confidering the daily and
rapid decline of the country, the amount of revenue, fo taken, will prove too much. The ftate of
the country, and of the people, calls as loudly for
abate-

abatement, as the necessities of the Company call for increase of revenue.

This, Sir, is the true way *to prevent corrupt or oppressive practices.* If you refer it to the servants abroad *to devise the methods,* and then to transmit their proceedings and determination to the Court of Directors for *their* final orders and directions : — in the first place, the delay of itself is a new, or, rather, a continued act of oppression to the natives ; but what is much worse, your measures are opposed to your experience :—you unnecessarily give powers, which you know, or ought to know, have been constantly abused. One example, if there were no other, ought to deter you from replacing a similar trust in similar hands. I have a right to assert, though not from my own knowledge, that the five-years settlement of the revenues of Bengal, made in the year 1772, *was sold* by the Committee of Circuit. The fact is notorious in India; but it is on the authority of the Court of Directors that I affirm it to be true. In their letter of the 4th of March, 1778, they ordered the Governor General and Council *forthwith to commence a profecution in the Supreme Court of Judicature against the persons who composed the Committee of Circuit, or their repre- sentatives *.*

I do not doubt that the subsequent clause, for securing the pensions allotted to some of the Zemin-

---

* This letter is signed by the present Chairman and Deputy Chairman of the Court of Directors, *Mr. Smith and Mr. Devaynes.*

dars

dars in lieu of their lands, was drawn up with a be-
nevolent intention; but I believe the fact it refers
to is misunderstood. The first and leading effort of
national justice should be to reinstate the proprietors, of every denomination, in the possession of
their property. The very measure, that forced these
pensions on the Zemindars, was an act of the most
despotic oppression. The rents demanded of them,
for this very purpose, were so high, that, rather
than be answerable for sums which they knew their
lands could not afford, they accepted of pensions,
and surrendered the possession and management of
their estates to strangers, to farmers, to adventurers,
to the banyans of the President and Council of Fort
William. Is it otherwise to be believed, that any
man in his senses would give up his landed estate for
a pension, to be held at the pleasure of an arbitrary
Government? — Do justice to these people, and
there will be no foundation for this clause.

It is proper and necessary that the Court of Directors should be restrained from sending any new
servant, civil or military, to India, until the establishments are fixed; and, when they are fixed, it
is equally proper that the Directors should be restrained from sending out writers, cadets, or others,
beyond the number necessary to fill up vacancies as
they happen. The service is overloaded with useless servants: they are a burthen to the Government,
and they constitute a tax of the worst sort upon the
country.

There

There seems to be no occasion for a law to confirm an existing rule of the Company's service. It is, and always has been, established, that promotions should be made according to seniority. The latitude given in the exception is perfectly unnecessary, as well as incorrectly worded *. The Governments abroad are ready enough to find *urgent occasion to deviate from the general rule.* The vote in Council is the very act of deviation, not the medium through which they see cause for it.

The next clause may properly be combined with another, which stands at a distance from it; I mean to consider the sixty-seventh and eighty-ninth clauses together. By the former no person, beyond a certain age, is to be sent to India as a cadet or writer ; but no reason for the limitation is assigned. By the latter, no person whatsoever, who shall have been employed, *in any capacity whatsoever*, in the East Indies, shall be capable of being appointed to any station or office in India, after he, having returned to this kingdom, shall have resided at home a certain time, unless it be proved that such residence was necessary for his health : so that the worst man in the service is capable of being reinstated, provided he resigned it on account of his health ; whereas an able and meritorious servant, who may have been obliged to come to England, and to reside here longer than the limited period, for the most urgent

---

* The terms of the exception are, " unless any of the said Go-
" vernments and Presidencies shall, on any very urgent occasion, by
" a vote in Council, see cause to deviate from the said general rule."

and

and juſtifiable reaſons, though not for ill health, is utterly prohibited from returning to a ſervice, to which he may have devoted his life, and for which he may have relinquiſhed all other proſpects and purſuits. I ſee no reaſon for the diſtinction. There is no poſitive merit in ſickneſs, though it has a natural claim to indulgence. One would think that the executive power of the Company, if the Court of Directors are equal to any of their duties, might ſafely be truſted with ſuch details as theſe. It is not an object that apparently requires the interpoſition of the Legiſlature : but if it did, the proper and uſeful regulation would be, not abſolutely to prohibit abſentees from returning to the ſervice, but to prevent their gaining rank in their abſence over thoſe, who continued to do their duty on the ſpot. Whoever ſtayed in England, beyond the limit of a reaſonable leave of abſence, ſhould return preciſely to the rank he held when he left India.

Taking the operation of the two clauſes together, the reſult ſeems to be, that, in the firſt inſtance, no man, who ſhall have acquired knowledge or experience in England, ſhall be permitted to go India ; and that no man, who may have acquired knowledge and experience in India, ſhall be permitted to return, unleſs his faculties have been ſufficiently impaired by his infirmities, to qualify him for reſuming the duties of his ſtation. The favourite idea ſeems to be, that youth and inexperience ſhould govern Bengal. An old maxim of policy attaches

E experience

experience to years, and wisdom to experience; and though I know there is a brilliant exception to, this maxim, I wish it to be left where it stands—a brilliant exception to a general principle, and not, that the exception should be converted into a rule.

Nothing can be objected to the principle and purpose of that clause, which makes all offences committed by British subjects in every other part of India, *or under pretence of the order of any native protected Prince*, amenable to the same laws, and liable to the same penalties, *as if they had been committed within the territories directly subject to the British Government*. At the same time, there will be a legal difficulty in the proceeding, which gentlemen of the profession would do well to consider. The process of our courts of justice does not run beyond the limits of our own provinces; so that, although the party accused may be in your power, the witnesses necessary to convict or acquit him cannot, in any regular course of proceeding, be compelled to appear. If this difficulty be not provided for, there can be no trial of the offences in question.

On the subject of presents, my opinion, perhaps, may be thought particular. Forms and appearances, I know, are against it. Undoubtedly the Governor General and Council, the Judges, and any others who have great established salaries, should derive no other advantage from their station. With respect to *them*, the prohibition of presents is proper; but it ought to be complete. I can assure the House, that the exception in favour of presents of ceremony
mony

mony *on solemn occasions*, is founded on ideas which I
know to be fallacious. The acceptance of ceremonial prefents is no way neceffary for fupporting the
dignity of men in power, nor has the refufal of them
ever given offence. General Clavering, Colonel
Monfon, and I, conftantly refufed them. We told
the natives, it was againft the law of England, the
very law by which we were appointed, and they
were fatisfied. Mr. Haftings declared, that he
fhould continue to receive *nuzzers*, and carry them
to the Company's account. Our other honourable
colleague, who is now a Member of the Houfe, *entirely approved of the honourable Prefident's conduct in
the receipt of complimentary nuzzers :* but he did not
equally approve of accounting for them to the Company. His words are ; " I might here make a ten-
" der to the Public of the trivial *nuzzers*, to the
" acceptance of which my ftation has impelled me.
" But what is proper for the Governor General,
" would in *me*, I apprehend, appear rather in the
" light of a confequential, infignificant difplay of
" rigidnefs in excefs!" In Mr. Haftings's letters
you have feen fome fplendid examples of the fub-
lime. The honourable gentleman, whofe words I
have juft repeated, fucceeds better in the profound.
It is his forte. Thefe trivial prefents accumulate
very faft. If I had laid myfelf out for the receipt
of them, I have no doubt, that while I was in
Bengal I might have realifed eight or nine thoufand
pounds from this petty fource of profit. To men
in high ftation, the prohibition fhould be abfolute.

In

In all ſtations, it ſhould be highly penal to receive money for corrupt purpoſes, or to extort it. In the ordinary tranſaction of buſineſs, I am inclined to think that preſents are not dangerous, and I know that they are uſeful. The Government of Bengal, through all its gradations, is a Government of favour, not of juſtice. Nothing would ever be done for the natives, if they did not gratify the perſons who forwarded their affairs. Whenever there ſhall be a Government of ſtrict juſtice in Bengal, and whenever proviſion ſhall be made for the various offices under it, proportioned to their reſpective rank and power, you may totally aboliſh preſents. Till then, you neither can, nor ought to do it — till then, the oaths you preſcribe to the collectors of the revenue will bind none but men of honour. Men of a different character will either totally diſregard the prohibition, or ſatisfy their ſcruples, if they have any, by accommodating the exception to all caſes, or all caſes to the exception. For the purpoſe of receiving *preſents of ceremony,* all occaſions will be found ſufficiently *ſolemn.*

By the ſixty-ninth clauſe, the whole gift or preſent is to be forfeited to the King : by the ſeventieth, the court of juſtice may order the gift to be reſtored to the party who gave it. Can the ſame preſent, ſuppoſing it were a diamond, be forfeited to the Crown and reſtored to the owner; or is it meant that the offender ſhall forfeit double the value in every inſtance ? — The two clauſes ſeem to me to contradict one another.

The

The seventy-first makes an exception in favour of counsellors at law, phyficians, furgeons, or chaplains; but it takes no notice of attornies, who are much more in the receipt of fees than any of the others.

With refpect to *the wilful difobeying, or the wilfully omitting to execute the Company's orders,* if there be no material inftances of the difobedience alluded to, the law that propofes to punifh it hereafter is fuperfluous and unjuft. The Legiflature interpofes before it is called upon : — it fuppofes offences, which are not ftated, and, by fuppofing them to exift generally, it confounds the innocent with the guilty. If they *do* exift, to a degree, that warrants and demands the interpofition of the Legiflature, they ought to be punifhed as well as forbidden ; at leaft the offenders ought to be removed from their places. When the laws prohibit on one fide, and perfect impunity encourages on the other, is it reafonable to expect that the prohibition fhould be regarded ? — The minds of men will be determined by what you *do*, not by what you *fay* ; and the more you threaten, the more you will be defpifed.

The two next claufes give a moft exorbitant and formidable power to the Governor General and Council, and to the fubordinate Prefidencies ; even to *Bencoolen !* — *All perfons fufpected of carrying on any illicit commerce or correfpondence* with any body, may be feized, imprifoned, and detained in cuftody by the Governor's warrant, until the Governor and Council fhall think fit to bring them to trial, or fend

them

them to England. No fact is stated, or even alluded to, that might require the delegation of so dangerous a trust. I declare, that while I was in India, there never was an instance fit to be named as the foundation of such a law as this; nor have I heard of any since. Correspondence with the enemies of the State is high treason; and treason may be punished without a new law. But what do you mean by *illicit commerce?* What transaction is there in life which an arbitrary Government may not interpret into *an illicit commerce?* Do you mean to deny the parties the benefit of the *Habeas Corpus?* Do you mean to leave it to the discretion of the Governor and Council at what time the party shall be tried, or to *their* option whether he shall be tried on the spot, or sent a prisoner to England? No, Sir; I know perfectly well what is meant. The liberty of every individual in India is to be held at the mercy of the Governor General. The clause has no real object, but to increase his personal power, and to make it irresistible.

. I have now gone through the second division of the bill. Before I proceed to the third, I have an appeal to make to the honour and to the justice of the House. It is of a nature so personal, that it will probaby excite their curiosity; but it is also connected with the public service. It has a natural and a necessary relation to the general object of the present bill, and therefore deserves their attention. It concerns the service of the public in future, that the character of men, who have faithfully

fully

fully and honourably difcharged the duties of a high ftation, fhould be protected from reproach. The infults, offered to the memory of fuch men, contribute to deter others from following their example, are injurious to the community, and ought to be refented with univerfal indignation. It is not of myfelf I fpeak;—that fpirit of prefumption does not belong to me. I am proud of the fortune, that connected my name and united my labours with thofe of Clavering and Monfon, and it is all the diftinction I pretend to.

When I fought to obtain a feat in the Houfe of Commons, it was not merely for the honour of fitting here, nor for any delight I take in your debates. With refpect to India affairs, my firft view was, not to ferve England or the India Company; but the natives of India if I could. To them I am bound by every obligation of juftice, gratitude, and compaffion. From *them* I received the falary, which gave me a fortune. But, even if the fervice of England had been my only object, this is the courfe I fhould have taken to purfue it. I will not appeal to your virtues, or fuppofe that you have any. If you have common fenfe, if, as interefted men, you understand your own intereft, you will treat the creatures, fubject to your power, with lenity and juftice. If wealth be your object, you will protect the induftry, you will nurfe and cherifh the eftate, by which you expect to be enriched.

My fecond reafon for obtaining a feat in Parliament was to have an opportunity of explaining my

own

own conduct, if it should be questioned, or defending it, if it should be attacked. The last, and not the least urgent reason was, that I might be ready to defend the character of my colleagues, not against specific charges, which I am sure will never be produced; but against the language of calumny, which endeavours to asperse, without daring to accuse. It is well known that a gross and public insult has been offered to the memory of General Clavering and Colonel Monson, by a person of high rank in this country. I was happy when I heard, that *my* name was included in it with theirs. So highly do I respect the character of those men, that I deem it an honour to share in the injustice it has suffered. — It is in compliance with the forms of the House, and not to shelter myself, or out of tenderness to the party, that I forbear to name him. I mean to describe him so exactly, that he cannot be mistaken. He declared in his place in a great assembly, and in the course of a grave deliberation, " that it would have been " happy for this country, if General Clavering, " Colonel Monson, and Mr. Francis, had been " drowned in their passage to India." — If this poor and spiteful invective had been uttered by a man of no consequence or repute, by any light, trifling, inconsiderate person, by a Lord of the Bedchamber for example, or any of the other silken Barons of modern days, I should have heard it with indifference. But when it is seriously urged and deliberately insisted on by a grave Lord of Parliament—

by

by a Judge,—by a man of ability and eminence in his profeffion, whofe perfonal difpofition is ferious, who carries gravity to fternefs, and fternefs to ferocity, it cannot be received with indifference, or anfwered without refentment. Such a man will be thought to have inquired before he pronounced. From *his* mouth, a reproach is a fentence, an invective is a judgement. — The accidents of life, and not any original diftinction that I know of, have placed *him* too high, and *me* at too great a diftance from him, to admit of any other anfwer from me, than a public defiance, for General Clavering, for Colonel Monfon, and for myfelf. This is not a party queftion, nor fhould it be left to fo feeble an advocate as I am to fupport it. — The friends and fellow foldiers of General Clavering and Colonel Monfon will affift me in defending their memory. I demand and expect the fupport of every man of honour in this Houfe, and in the kingdom. What character is fafe, if flander be permitted to attack the reputation of two of the moft honourable and virtuous men that ever were employed, or ever perifhed in the fervice of their country? — I know that the authority of this man is not without weight; but I have an infinitely higher authority to oppofe to it. I had the happinefs of hearing the merits of General Clavering and Colonel Monfon acknowledged and applauded in terms, to which I am not at liberty to do more than to allude. They were rapid and expreffive. I muft not venture to repeat leaft I fhould do them injuftice, or violate

F   the

the forms of respect, where essentially I owe and feel the most. But I am sufficiently understood. The generous sensations, that animate the Royal mind, are easily distinguished from those, which rankle in the heart of that person, who is supposed to be the keeper of the Royal conscience.

The third division of the bill includes the institution of a new judicature, avowedly repugnant to all the principles of the criminal jurisprudence of this country, and of which there is no example, but the Star Chamber, in the history of England. My surprise and disappointment, when I heard this part of the bill recommended and insisted on by the Chancellor of the Exchequer, are not to be expressed. Yet I might have been in some degree prepared for the event. This is not the first instance, in which I have observed that the right honourable gentleman is never more urgent, is never more eloquent in establishing the truth of a general proposition, or in exalting the virtues of a general principle, than at the moment he is going to introduce an exception to it. — No man, who heard him, can have forgotten, how earnestly and how vehemently he recommended it to the House, not to let their anxiety for the better government of India, however laudable, engage them to do any thing inconsistent with the security of our own domestic establishment, or that might directly or indirectly intrench on our own constitution. From this general caution, he proceeded to a warm and animated panegyric of the trial by jury. I declare most solemnly

lemnly that I thought he was going to new model the Supreme Court of Judicature at Calcutta, and to reſtore the Britiſh ſubjeĉts in India to their birthright, of which they were deprived by the charter of that Court, for no good purpoſe that I can diſcover, but certainly without any good effeĉt. When the right honourable gentleman had thus eſtabliſhed his premiſes, by an appeal to conſtitutional topics, which always gain upon an Engliſh audience, he turned ſhort to a concluſion, which I imagine muſt have diſappointed and aſtoniſhed every man, who was not immediately in the ſecret—" That the " beſt general rules were ſubjeĉt to exceptions, that " neceſſity created a law of its own, and that ſuch " a neceſſity exiſted at preſent. That the puniſh- " ment of Indian delinquents could not be obtain- " ed by proceedings in Parliament, nor by proſe- " cution in the courts of common law,—of courſe " that there was no alternative, but to create a ſpe- " cial judicature, with ſummary proceedings, *and* " *without the intervention of a Jury*, for the trial of " offences committed in India."—In the firſt place, Sir, I deny the ſuppoſition, on which the inference is founded. I have no doubt that delinquency of every kind may be effeĉtually tried and puniſhed by the judicatures that exiſt. But if I thought otherwiſe,— if I were perfeĉtly convinced that Indian delinquents could no way be puniſhed but by a violent innovation in the criminal law of the kingdom, I would not purchaſe their puniſhment at ſo ruinous an expence. I would not, for the ſake of that ob-

jeĉt,

ject, though I think it important, consent to a breach of any kind in the principal barrier of the freedom of England. When the precedent is established, I know not what farther innovations may be gradually grafted upon it, or how rapidly it may advance to the destruction of those principles, which it begins with invading. We are not yet however reduced to that consideration. Let us try whether, in effect, the right honourable gentleman is warranted in affirming that there is no alternative. If there be, the principles we both profess oblige him to prefer it. — I am but little of a lawyer, and I am very desirous to be instructed. If I should be mistaken in my facts, some of the learned gentlemen opposite to me will have the goodness to correct me.

Supposing it to be admitted, that taking the law as it now stands, the formality of pleading, and the difficulty of ascertaining, according to the strict rules of evidence, facts which have arisen beyond sea, are such as will create a failure of justice, it does not follow, that it is at all necessary to deprive persons accused of offences in India of trial by Jury. The Court of King's Bench has already the power of trying misdemeanors committed in India, under the 13th of Geo. III. cap. 63. *with the assistance of a Jury.* If the forms of pleading and the rules of evidence stand in the way of justice, let the law be altered : — with respect to special pleading and evidence, let the King's Bench be governed by the same rules that are laid down to govern the practice of this new Court ; and then it will be as com‐

petent

petent as this can be, to take cognizance of, and
punish offences committed in India, and still the party accused will, in every instance, have the privilege of being tried by his peers. When the act of
1774 was made, it was thought necessary to alter
the law with regard to evidence : and it was accordingly enacted, that depositions, taken under a commission in India, should be admitted as evidence in
the King's Bench; but trial by jury still remained.
The Legislature did nothing to affect that mode of
trial. Before that act, a misdemeanor committed
in India could not have been tried upon an information in the King's Bench, so that here was a new
jurisdiction given to that Court ; its jurisdiction
was at least extended to offences in India, which
were before not cognizable in that Court, either by
information or indictment. At common law, trea-
sons committed out of the realm were not punish-
able in England. To remedy this defect, various
acts were made in the reign of Henry VIII. : but
even in the arbitrary reign of that Monarch, no attempt was made to deprive the subject of trial by
jury. At common law, murders committed in foreign parts could not be inquired into in England ;
but by the 33d Henry VIII. cap. 23. they might be
inquired of, and tried by the King's *special commission* in England. By that act a *new tribunal* was
erected ; but still no attempt was made to abolish
trial by jury. Even in that *commission* court, the
party had the privilege of being tried by his peers.
If it be true, that a new species of criminality makes

a new

a new courfe of proceeding unavoidable, the ground of the diftinction muft be fairly and clearly eftablifhed. The anfwer I expect muft not be technical, but plain enough to fatisfy the underftanding of men, who are not learned. When the common intereft is at ftake, the common fenfe of the nation fhould be confulted.

A word or two more on the general fituation of the country, and I have done. We have it from the authority of a noble Lord*, or rather of a noble convert, whofe opinions very properly bend to his experience, that, at a former period, he had oppofed the prefent Adminiftration, becaufe he difapproved of the courfes, by which they had poffeffed themfelves of power ; — that the cafe was *now* completely altered ; that the fenfe of the nation had been unanimoufly declared, and that the united voice of the nation could not be refifted ; — that the Minifter had *now* come into power, *at the front door of the Houfe, and on the fhoulders of the People.* I do not mean to difpute the truth of thefe propofitions, much lefs the propriety of any change of opinion, that may be founded upon them. Take the fact as it is ftated, and compare it with the confequences, which it has immediately produced. Wherever fenfation exifts, the comparifon will be felt ; and, if men are ftill capable of reflection, it will force them to reflect. The very firft act of this popular Adminiftration, of a Minifter, who comes into power *on the fhoulders of the People,* attacks the Democracy

* Lord Delaval.

of the country, and annihilates the firſt of all the popular powers of the Conſtitution. The deciſion of the queſtion upon the Weſtminſter election, however it may be turned, or in whatever colours it may be dreſſed, carries you finally and inevitably to this concluſion ; that the People of Great Britain *may* be governed by laws, to which they have not conſented, and *may* be taxed by a Houſe of Commons, in which they are not repreſented. If this be the fact of Weſtminſter to-day, why not of London to-morrow, — of Middleſex the next ? On the face of the precedent, I ſee nothing to confine it.

The ſecond meaſure of this popular Adminiſtration attacks the trial by jury, and threatens to aboliſh it. Such are the inſtant operations of that very power, which pretends to be derived from the confidence of the People. — But if the People of England are not mad as well as blind, if they have not loſt their underſtanding as well as their feelings, they will ſoon ſee how unwiſely they have beſtowed their confidence, and repent of their deluſion, when repentance is too late.

HOUSE

HOUSE OF COMMONS.

MONDAY, July 27, 1784.

" THE order of the day being read, for taking
" into further confideration the Report from the
" Committee of the whole Houfe, to whom the
" Bill for the better regulation and management of
" the affairs of the Eaft-India Company, and of the
" Britifh poffeffions in India, and for eftablifhing a
" Court of Judicature for the more fpeedy and
" effectual trial of perfons accufed of offences in
" the Eaft Indies, was committed."

Mr. FRANCIS.

Mr. SPEAKER,

My objections to the bill, as it now ftands, are in
fome refpects changed; but they are very little di-
minifhed. It is not to be denied, that the bill has
been materially altered, and, in fome inftances, improved in the Committee. Inftead of profeffing
candour, which too often is affectation, I fhall
fpeak

speak of the present merits of the bill, with sincerity. I allow that several clauses have been prudently corrected, and others very properly omitted; but I do not mean to admit, that particular improvements, grafted on false principles, can essentially mend the measure. It is possible that a thing, which is wrong in one extreme, may be equally wrong in another. In acknowledging the improvements that have been made, I hope at least to establish a claim to credit, when I return to my objections.

No orders are now to be sent to India by the Commissioners without the knowledge of the Directors, or to the Commanders in Chief in India, without the knowledge of the respective Presidencies. Orders of every kind are now to be conveyed through the proper constitutional channels. While you suffer the Court of Directors to exist, their authority belongs to the constitution of the Company, To pass by the first is to destroy the second. The absurdity of that idea is acknowledged and corrected. The clauses, by which the appointment of the several Commanders in Chief, and of persons to succeed to the command in case of vacancy, was to be given to His Majesty, are omitted. Undoubtedly, nothing could be more extravagant than the idea of separating the military from the civil power of the Company's Government. The alteration was indispensably necessary. At the same time, I have no conception how it can possibly be reconciled to a political principle, which a right honourable gentleman, in opening the

G   original

original plan of the bill, laid down as fundamental.
He urged and infisted on the truth of this propofition, and afferted it to be inherent in the Englifh
conftitution, that the armies of any one State, however they might be divided, or wherever they might
be employed, belonged to the department of the
executive power, and that therefore the appointment
to the feveral commands of the Company's forces
fhould unqueftionably be vefted in the Crown. He
had then forgotten, what he poffibly may fince have
recollected, that the Court of Directors are in fact
the executive power of the State in queftion. But
I need not combat a propofition, which he himfelf
has fo completely abandoned. The right honourable gentleman, I fee, is not obftinately tenacious of
his principles, or his complaifance to his friends muft
be unbounded.

The feveral claufes in the original bill, which relate to the private debts of the Nabob of Arcot
and the Rajah of Tanjore ;— the refpective claims
or undetermined rights and pretenfions of thofe
princes ;— the reinftatement of difpoffeffed Rajahs,
Zemindars, and other landholders ;—the fixation of
the rents or tributes to be paid in future ; — the reduction of expences, and the final limitation of efta-
blifhments, offices, and emoluments ;—are all completely relinquifhed, — I will not prefume to fay, in
compliance with *my* opinion, but a good deal in
conformity to it. — The principle I recommended
feems to be generally adopted, that whatever can be
done, immediately by the Directors at home, fhould

not

not be referred to the fervants abroad. Yet I am forry to fee that, in this general fweep, the very beft claufe of the firft bill is included. I mean the one marked 58, by which it was provided " that it " fhould not be lawful for the Governor General " and Council of Fort William, or the Governor " and Council of any of the other Prefidencies, or " any fervant or agent of the faid United Com- " pany, of what defcription or denomination foever, " to alter fuch tribute, rent, fervice, or payment " as the faid Court of Directors fhould have finally " confirmed, upon any pretence whatfoever, or to " exact from or impofe upon any native Prince, or " his heirs, or perfons claiming under them, any " greater or different tribute, rent, fervice, or pay- " ment, than fuch as fhould have been confirmed " by the Court of Directors."

I moft earneftly recommend it to the right ho- nourable gentleman to reinftate this claufe, or to revive the fpirit of it, in terms accommodated to the new principle which appears to be affumed. The tribute once fixed, I would not leave it in the power even of the Directors to alter it.

The claufe, refpecting prefents, is properly amended. Wherever the prohibition is right, it ought to ftand without exception. Admitting that prefents were really and purely ceremonial, in *my* mind they degrade the dignity of a high ftation inftead of exalting it. What in fact, and even in appearance, can be more difgraceful, than for a Britifh Governor to hold out his hand to receive a

G 2 few

few gold mohrs or rupees from every native, who comes to vifit him, and frequently from perfons, who are unable to afford it. The true dignity of power is to be acceffible to its fubjects, without expecting them to pay for it. With refpect to the fubordinate ranks of the fervice, I ftill have my doubts. I am perfectly fatisfied, that in the prefent ftate of the fervice, no law can prevent the practice, and I am not fure that you ought to attempt it. I have no expectation that fuch a direct provifion will ever be made for the Company's fervants, as will even afford them a fubfiftence ; much lefs an exceeding, out of which an independence can be gradually accumulated, by any efforts of œconomy. People in England have no idea of the expence of living in Bengal. There is no fuch thing as commerce. The few, who have engaged in enterprifes of internal induftry, have either totally failed, or been obliged to abandon them :— and the falaries, given by the Company, below the Board of Trade and the Colonels of Brigades, are very inconfiderable. Yet no man fhould be cut off from the hopes of a reafonable and moderate independence, in proportion to his ftation.— Human inftitutions fhould confult human nature.

I believe, Sir, I have now taken notice of every material amendment, that deferves commendation. The other branches of the fubject are more numerous and productive.

In comparing the prefent bill with the firft, there is one general preliminary obfervation to be made

upon

upon them both ; that the two bills draw two con-
clusions equally false, though perfectly different,
from one and the fame false principle of policy.
The principle, common to them both, is, that,
where power is really wanted, where power ought
to be strengthened, the sureft way to ftrengthen it
will be to divide it. On this foundation, the firft
bill, instead of uniting the executive powers of the
Company in any one Board, divided them between
the Commiffioners and the Directors, with fo great a
preponderance in favour of the former, that the
latter in reality were reduced to nothing and ought
to have been abolished. On the fame foundation,
the present bill continues to divide a power, which
ought to be united, but diftributes it differently. The
Crown and the Commiffioners furrender almoft every thing they had taken, and the Directors are re-
invested with a power, which evidently fuppofes
them fit to be highly trufted. But the truft, as it
ftands, is incompatible with the control. The firft
bill, placing no confidence in the Directors, divefted
them of all power. The amended bill continues
a check, in which the fame want of confidence is
implied, yet reftores them to a power, which ought
never to be given to men who are diftrufted. —
With refpect to the governments abroad, the means
taken to accomplish the profeffed object of both the
bills are nearly the fame. In order to make the
power at home more capable of governing, they
divide it. But, in order to make the power in India more governable, they ftrengthen and unite it.
This

This is the fenſe, in which the old maxim, *divide et impera*, is now underſtood. This is the way, in which ancient maxims of policy are interpreted and applied by modern politicians.

The amended bill reduces the Preſidency of Fort William to a Governor General and three Counſellors, for the immediate purpoſe, *expreſsly avowed* by the Chancellor of the Exchequer, of giving effect to the caſting voice, in order to increaſe and ſtrengthen the power of the Governor General. This, I believe, is the firſt example of ſuch a uſe and application of the effect of a caſting voice. In all deliberative councils and aſſemblies whatever, the true and natural principle of deciſion is by a real majority of votes. But numbers, who debate, may diſagree; and, if the whole number happens to be even, they may poſſibly divide into equal parts. In that caſe only, the operation of the caſting voice is made uſe of to create a fictitious majority, not for the purpoſe of giving power, but merely to obtain a deciſion. — Hitherto the caſting voice has been conſidered as a neceſſary proviſion againſt a poſſible inconvenience. The preſent bill creates the inconvenience, not merely for the purpoſe of correcting it, but to convey a power, which, if proper to be given at all, ought to be given by a direct courſe, and ſecured againſt accidents. On the principle of the clauſes in queſtion, the Governor General ought to be a diſtinct perſon, and veſted with powers independent of the Council. — As long as a Council of four is full, the whole power, that belongs to it,

will

will certainly veft in the Prefident, provided he has fkill enough to fecure the blind and devoted fupport of any one of the other three; and this, I know, may be done. But, fuppofe his complaifant friend fhould die or depart, and the other two fhould continue obftinate;—the declared object of the bill is defeated.—The Prefident is reduced to a ftate, in which he can do nothing but perplex or embarrafs the others, and in that ftate he muft remain, until his intereft and influence at home fhall have accomplifhed another appointment. A year and a half at leaft muft elapfe, before his new colleague can come to his affiftance.—If therefore the power be proper, the bill fhould take care to provide for its being held and exercifed without interruption.—Sir, I am not fuppofing imaginary cafes. The oppofition to Mr. Haftings has not been confined to General Clavering, Colonel Monfon, and myfelf. His prefent colleagues, Mr. Wheler, Mr. Macpherfon, and Mr. Stables, have exactly the fame opinion, that we had, of him and of his meafures. Their oppofition is as vigorous as *they* can make it, and, I believe, more deeply refented by Mr. Haftings, than ours.—From *our* oppofition, however it might diftrefs him, he felt no degradation. Of his prefent colleagues I know he has written home to this effect, that he fhould have quitted the Government long ago, if he could have ventured to leave it in *fuch* hands as *theirs!*

But perhaps it may be fufpected that the Chancellor of the Exchequer, in forming this arrangement,
ment,

ment, has been guided by experience, and that he has facts of importance to appeal to in support of it. —I will tell the House how the facts stand, and leave it to their judgement to compare them with the arrangement. Some of the Directors are present, and I call upon them to support me if I am right, or to contradict me if I am wrong.

Before the death of Colonel Monson, the Council consisted of five persons. I do not mean at present to inquire into the respective merits of the two parties, into which it was divided, or to exalt one at the expence of the other. For the immediate purpose of the present argument, it is sufficient for me to say, what every man in India and in the direction knows to be true, that, while the Government of Bengal was in the hands of five persons, the Company's affairs were prudently conducted, and prospered accordingly. The system, laid down in their general instructions, was observed; — their orders were obeyed; — their debts were discharged; — their treasury was filled; — and great investments were provided by savings out of the revenue. Above all the rest, *we fixed our attention to the preservation of peace throughout India.* We maintained it ourselves, and, when it was violated by the Presidency of Bombay, we restored it by a direct interposition of the authority of our Government. When the death of Colonel Monson had reduced the Council to four, which it seems is now the favourite number, the mischiefs, which have since desolated India and ruined the India Company, began to operate. The second

second war with the Marattas was planned at Bombay the moment they heard of the death of General Clavering, and received, embraced, and promoted by the Governor General and Council, the moment the plan was communicated to us. In lefs than five months after the death of General Clavering, the resolution was taken at Fort William to break the definitive treaty of peace concluded but a year before at *Poorundur*, and to send an army acrofs India to invade the *Pefhwa*'s dominions. The General's place was soon supplied by Mr. Wheler, fo that, from Colonel Monfon's death in October 1776, to the arrival of Sir Eyre Coote in March 1779, the Council confifted of four perfons, excepting an interval of three or four months, in which I ftood alone againft Mr. Haftings and Mr. Barwell; and in that period, I affirm that all the mifchiefs, with which you are now oppreffed, took their birth, and grew into effects, which by this time, I fear, are not to be retrieved.—Your treafuries are empty;— your debts are infupportable;—your inveftment, when you have any, is paid for by bills on the Company, and two thirds of India have been laid wafte. With thefe facts before you, is it poffible for the Legiflature to reject the number, under which the Company's affairs were wifely and happily conducted in India, and voluntarily prefer that, under which every thing has been done, which this very law profeffes to condemn, and moft ftrongly prohibits?

. . By the feventeenth and eighteenth claufes of the amended bill, the fituation of a Commander in Chief of all the Company's forces in India is now provided for. At laft it has been difcovered, that fuch an office exifts. I have no objeftion to the voice and precedence given him in the Supreme Council, or at the fubordinate Councils of Fort St. George and Bombay, when he fhall happen to be at either of them. — But I ftrongly objeft to the fituation, in which his arrival there will place the refpeftive Commanders in Chief at thofe two Prefidencies. He not only fuperfedes them in rank, but reduces them to filence. During *his* ftay, they are only to have a feat, but no voice, in the Council. The Houfe will obferve that this is a civil office, not a military command; but, even on the ftrifteft military ideas, the provifion is abfurd. The arrival of a fuperior officer difpoffeffes the inferior, but does not annihilate him; he ftill continues fecond in command, with a real and effeftive, though not with an equal authority. For what reafon he is inftantly to be converted into a mute, I cannot conceive. Naturally he ought to be better informed than a ftranger concerning the affairs of the Prefidency, where he has commanded. But the objeft of the claufe is to filence the perfon, who, having the beft information, ought to be fpecially confulted. It ought to be confidered too, whether gentlemen of high rank in the army, whether a general officer in the King's fervice, who may happen to command upon the coaft, be likely to fubmit to this fort of

treatment,

treatment, or how far it may wound the honourable feelings and spirit of the profession?

Sir, I shall leave the remaining regulations of the bill to other gentlemen, who I believe have considered them with proper attention, and go at once to that article, which, I confefs, is to me more important than all the reft. I mean the new judicature, which the bill introduces into the criminal law of this country. I perceive that, in the apprehenfion of fome gentlemen, this part of the bill has been confiderably corrected and improved by the amendments made in the Committee, and that fome gentlemen, who objected to it at firft, are now fatisfied. I am truly forry for it; becaufe I wifh that the principle of every meafure, which I deem to be dangerous to the conftitution, fhould appear at once to the public view, undifguifed, in its real fhape, and in the colours that belong to it. *They* deceive themfelves groffly who imagine that that, which is effentially wrong, can ever be formally right. It cannot be corrected or improved, becaufe the defect is in the effence, not in the form. And why fhould you lay afide the trial by jury in the cafe of Indian delinquents? I have yet heard no one affirmative reafon affigned for it. Is it fufpected that a Jury will not do juftice? You have no ground for the fufpicion; on the contrary, in the only cafe in point, in the only cafe of Indian delinquency that has been profecuted in a court of common law, the Jury did their duty. I do not mean to enter into the merits of the profecution of Mr. Stratton and Mr. Brooke for

difdispoffeffing and imprisoning Lord Pigot ; it is sufficient for my present purpose to say, that the public in general thought that those persons deserved to be severely punished, and expected that they would be so. Why were they not ? The Jury did *their* part in finding them guilty. If they were not sufficiently punished, it was the fault of the Bench. Now, observe the consequence : You lay aside the Jury, who, in the only instance in point, did every thing that depended on them to bring the criminals to condign punishment, and you think you are sure of justice, in uniting the incompatible offices of Judge and Jury in the same persons, who, the only time they were tried, have totally disappointed the public expectation of public justice. But all reason and argument are useless against power. If a British House of Commons can, on any terms, consent, in any instance, to abolish the trial by Jury, and if the people at large are insensible of the danger of such a precedent, individuals, who have done their duty, must submit to their share in the mischief, which they could not prevent. I fear the temper and character of the nation are changed. Though I am not an old man, I can remember a time, when an attempt of this nature would have thrown the whole kingdom into a flame. Had it been made when a great man *, who is now no more, had a seat in this House, he would have started from the bed of sickness, he would have solicited some friendly hand to depofit

* he late Earl of Chatham.

him

him on this floor, and from this station, with a monarch's voice, would have called the kingdom to
arms to oppose it. But *he* is dead, and has left
nothing in this world, that resembles him. He is
dead, and the sense, and honour, and character,
and understanding of the nation are dead with him.
But it seems there is a *necessity*, that supersedes all
objections. Justice must be done, and criminals
must be punished. Sir, it requires some fortitude;
it requires patience, long exercised, to endure so
gross a mockery. The bill, that threatens future
punishment to future crimes, gives you a special
earnest of its sincerity, in sheltering every offence,
and protecting every offender who has hitherto
existed, or who does exist at this hour. The present law opens its bosom to receive them, and
there they are safe : nay, it carries its precaution
farther; it provides for the security of crimes *in
esse*, that are actually unfinished, and allows a sufficient time, in which they may be compleated.
When these honourable services are accomplished,
strict Justice is then to take her seat. From that
moment we are never to see any thing but her sword.
When the whole harvest has been plundered, when
the field itself has been trampled into dust, you
denounce racks and gibbets to the petty larceny,
that hereafter may glean a few ears of corn. I
have done my part to the utmost of my little judgement and ability. From those, to whom more has
been given, more will be expected. What I have
said will not be useless, if it suggests the materials
of

of reflection to others, and furnishes employment for greater abilities.

The other regulations of the bill may be thought to require immediate difpatch. If they are proper to be executed at all, they cannot be carried too foon into effect. But no argument of that kind can be applied to the claufes, that regard the Judicature. The bill, on the face of it, expreffes no particular hurry to punifh any body. — For what poffible reafon then, fhould this part of the bill be fo urgently preffed forward to keep pace with the reft ? — The prefent Adminiftration, we are told, poffeffes the confidence, and are at all times ready to appeal to the judgement of the People. Let us fee whether they are ready to act up to their profeffions. Surely, Sir, there never can be an occafion more proper for an appeal to the fenfe of the nation, than when Government is going to introduce a new mode of trial into the law of this land, which, in the firft inftance, deprives a part of the people of their common right, and which, on fimilar pretences, may be extended to the whole kingdom. If the nation acquiefces, you lofe nothing by the delay. If not, you are bound by your principles to relinquifh the attempt.

Allow me a word at parting to an honourable *, and a learned † gentleman : to one of whom I am much indebted, and to the other, fpecially engaged. The honourable gentleman affures the Houfe, that

* Major John Scott, member for Weftloo.
† Henry Dundas, Efq. member for Edinburghfhire.

he is not the reprefentative of Mr. Haftings, though a confiderable part of his life be employed in attacking, defending, and refenting for that gentleman. I obferve it to his credit, that, although he is not a principal in thefe queftions, he takes part in them with no lefs activity and zeal, than if the caufe were directly and effentially his own. Between the honourable gentleman and me there is not, nor ever has been, any perfonal fubject of offence. In one fenfe therefore, I may be permitted to confider him as the reprefentative of Mr. Haftings, fince every man of honour is properly the reprefentative of an abfent friend. This, I prefume, was the principle, on which the honourable gentleman muft have acted, when he very lately created an opportunity of reciting to the Houfe fome tedious paffages from a letter of ten years ftanding, which, pronouncing it to be extremely dull, he naturally, and I cannot fay unwarrantably, concluded to be mine. But his eagernefs to punifh the guilty, made him forget that the Houfe was innocent. The honourable gentleman had no mercy upon either. Not confining himfelf to my fuppofed writings, he thought it a good opportunity to produce fome ferious charges againft my conduct. To thefe laft, my anfwer upon the inftant, I believe was thought fufficient. My own feelings affured me, that I carried the fenfe of the Houfe along with me. To his affertion, that we went to India pre-determined to declare war with Mr. Haftings at the moment of our arrival, I faid, that the moment of our arrival gave us an

insight

infight into his conduct, which made it impoffi-
blo for us, as honeft men, to unite with him.
Contrary to all his own repeated declarations and
profeffions refpecting a pacific fyftem, we found
the Company's army engaged by him in the extirpation of the Rohilla nation, with whom we had
lately been in alliance, and with whom the Englifh
had no quarrel whatever, for the fole and acknowledged purpofe of gaining a fum of money. We
found he had fold the extirpation of a whole
people, who had never offended us, for forty
lacks of rupees ; not a rupee of which had
been paid, though the fervice was compleated.
We found a third part of the whole military force
of Bengal had marched to places, fo remote from
our own territory, that none of the ordinary maps
of Hindoftan went far enough north to include their
fituation. I fubmit to judgement, whether thefe
facts alone did not oblige us to alter our opinion,
not only of Mr. Haftings's political conduct, but of
his perfonal character. The prejudices we carried
with us to India were paffionately and almoft ab-
furdly in his favour. I need not enter farther into
the merits of a queftion, on which every tribunal,
that was competent to examine it, has formally pronounced condemnation againft him. On the 28th
of November, 1775, the Court of Directors unanimoufly refolved, " That the agreement made with
" Sujah Dowlah, and the then Governor, (Mr.
" Haftings) for the hire of a part of the Compa-
" ny's troops for the reduction of the Rohilla coun-
" try,

" try, and the fubfequent fteps taken for the car-
" rying on that war, were founded on wrong poli-
" cy, were contrary to the general orders of the
" Company, for keeping the troops within the
" bounds of the provinces, and for not extending
" their conquefts; and were alfo contrary to *thofe*
" *general principles of juftice,* which the Company
" wifh fhould be fupported."

Even his fpecial friends the Proprietors, on this
occafion concurred with the Directors. Except that
he had intereft enough in that quarter to get the re-
ference to *juftice* omitted, the whole body of the
Proprietors, *und voce,* condemned him. On the
6th of December, 1775, they refolved unanimoufly,
" That notwithftanding this Court hath the higheft
" opinion of the fervices and integrity of Warren
" Haftings, Efq. and cannot admit a fufpicion of
" corrupt motives operating on his conduct with-
" out proof; yet they are of opinion, with their
" Court of Directors, that the agreement made
" with Sujah Dowlah for the hire of a part of the
" Company's troops for the reduction of the Ro-
" hilla country, and the fubfequent fteps taken for
" carrying on that war, were founded on wrong
" policy, were contrary to the general orders of the
" Company frequently repeated, for keeping their
" troops within the bounds of the provinces, and
" for not extending their territories; and were alfo
" contrary to thofe general principles, which the
" Company wifh fhould be fupported."

I   The

The honourable gentleman was then pleafed to charge me with having oppofed General Clavering on a particular occafion, but with fo much apparent reluctance, and in terms of fo much doubt and apprehenfion, as evidently betrayed the dependence of my fituation. A difference of opinion feems a ftrange proof of dependance. He concluded however that I was bound by fome fecret inftructions to follow the dictates of General Clavering, and that, when I refufed to be guided by him, I hazarded my employment. This, indeed, if it were true, would be a ferious charge not only againft me, but againft General Clavering himfelf, whofe memory the honourable gentleman profeffes to refpect, and againft the noble Lord * in the blue ribband, by whom alone fuch inftructions could have been given. The honourable gentleman, however, has in fome degree anfwered his own charge. Forgetting every thing that he had faid of my fuppofed dependence on my colleagues, he almoft in the fame breath affured the Houfe, that, with refpect to General Clavering and Colonel Monfon, I was *primus inter pares,* and that being at the head of a majority, I had in effect the whole government in my hands. If that be true, my colleagues were no more than cyphers at my difpofal. But in reality, the charge and the defence are equally trifling. I differed with General Clavering, not once but often, as the honourable gentleman will find, if he will look over our proceed-

* Lord North.

ings.

ings. Men of real honour, though generally united, and acting together on the fame general principles, will often difagree, and when they difagree, will be ready to declare it. Men of a different character, uniting on a different principle, will never difagree in particulars, as long as their general engagement to each other fubfifts. It is perfectly true that I felt and expreffed the utmoft anxiety at differing from General Clavering on a queftion of importance; but not for the reafon fufpected by the honourable gentleman. I dreaded the conftruction, which ignorance and malignity would be ready enough to give to my concurring with Mr. Haftings. I knew my fituation. When I oppofed him, it was faction. When I concurred with him, it was corruption. The honourable gentleman, however, has omitted a material part of the ftory. He has inadvertently neglected to inform the Houfe that the Court of Directors, in their letter of the 5th of February 1777, *intirely agreed* with *me* on the point in queftion.

The honourable gentleman fays that we fhould have acted wifely for the public fervice, if, inftead of looking back to the errors of former times, we had drawn a veil over every thing that was paft, and directed our efforts to future improvement. Sir, I am not of that opinion. I have no idea that fuch a plan would have been practicable, and I am fure it would have been unjuft. Injuftice is not valid becaufe it has been done. We could not abfolutely fhut our ears to complaints. We could not fay,

I 2 that

that no man, who had been injured, fhould ever be redreffed. The Supreme Court of Judicature looked very far back indeed, when it was their object to make an example, and to hold it out to the natives. But if the contrary had been true ; — if the honourable gentleman's abftract opinion were ever judicious, he forgets that we had no choice. He forgets that the Court of Directors prefcribed to us the very conduct we obferved, and applauded us highly for purfuing it.

The only point, on which I could not inftantly recollect enough of the fubject to give the honourable gentleman an immediate anfwer, regarded the reprefentation, which he fays, I drew up in December 1774, of the condition of Bengal at that time. He charges me with a wild exaggeration in faying, that Bengal, even then, was *reduced to the hazard of beggary and ruin.* Sir, a mere queftion of perfonal debate between the honourable gentleman and me, would be of too little moment, even to ourfelves, to be obtruded on the Houfe, if it did not lead to information immediately connected with the general fubject-matter of our prefent deliberation. You are going to make a law for the better government of Bengal. It is therefore proper you fhould inquire, what the ftate of Bengal was ten years ago, when the Legiflature firft interpofed for the fame purpofe. The Houfe fhould next endeavour to poffefs itfelf of the events, which have happened in the interval, and then

then you will be able to determine, what is probably the actual state of the object, concerning which you are going to exercise your legiflative power.

The Houfe, I imagine, will hear with furprife, that the firft intimation I received of the diftrefs of the Government of Fort William, was in a private converfation with Mr. Haftings himfelf. On evidence of this kind, I certainly fhould think it improper to infift, if it had not concurred with many recorded declarations made by Mr. Haftings to the fame effect. The fundamental argument conftantly ufed by him in defence of the Rohilla war, was, the diftrefs of the Company's affairs both at home and abroad. In his minute of the 3d December, 1774, he fays,

" All our advices, both public and private, re-
" prefented the diftreffes of the Company at home,
" as extreme. At the fame time, fuch was the
" ftate of affairs in this Government, that for many
" years paft, the income of the year was found in-
" adequate to its expence, to defray which, a hea-
" vy bond debt, amounting at one time to a hun-
" dred and twenty-five lacks of rupees, had accu-
" mulated. By allowing the Vizier the military
" aid, which he required, a faving of near one
" third of our military expences would be effected
" during the period of fuch a fervice, and the fti-
" pulation of forty lacks would afford an ample
" fupply to our treafury, and to the currency of the
" country."

On

- On this declaration, our firſt obſervation was, *that urgent diſtreſs was implied in the violent nature of the remedy.*

The maxims of policy invented by Mr. Haſtings to ſupport the fact, accommodate themſelves perfectly to the motives on which he acted.

30th Nov. 1774.

" If the internal reſources of a ſtate fail it, or " are not equal to its occaſional wants, whence can " it obtain immediate relief, but from external " means ?"

30th Nov. 1774.

" I ſhall be always ready to profeſs, that I do " reckon the probable acquiſition of wealth among " my reaſons for taking up arms againſt my *neigh-* " *bours.*"

Obſerve, Sir, that one of Mr. Haſtings's motives for taking up arms againſt his *neighbours*, not againſt his *enemies*, is plainly and explicitly to get poſſeſſion of their wealth.

· With reſpect to the actual diſtreſs of the Government and country of Bengal, I deſire nothing to be believed on my own aſſertion. On the 17th of October, 1774, a day or two before our arrival at Calcutta, Mr. Haſtings and his Council drew up a letter to the Court of Directors in defence of the Rohilla war, which they principally reſted on " the " acquiſition of forty lacks of rupees to the Com- " pany, and of ſo much ſpecie added *to the ex-* " *hauſted currency of theſe provinces :*" not a rupee

of

of which, however, was received until some time after our arrival.

With respect to the internal state of the provinces, I presume that the evidence of the late Mr. Samuel Middleton, one of the oldest and most experienced of the Company's servants in Bengal, will be allowed to be conclusive. If it were not, I could support it by a mass of other evidence of equal authority. In his letter of the 5th of February 1775, near five months after our arrival, he says, " When " a very considerable portion, supposed even a third " of the whole inhabitants, had perished, the re- " maining two thirds were obliged to pay for the " lands now left without cultivators. The country " has languished ever since, *and the evil continues* " *enhancing every day.*" Now, Sir, I think it will be admitted, that no description of national or political distress can easily be exaggerated, which is founded on evidence and authorities such as these. But has any thing happened, since that time, to improve the state of the country? — Excepting the short interval, in which General Clavering's principles and authority prevailed, have you heard of any thing but war in all parts of India? — But the oppression and rebellion of Princes subject to your power? — Mutinies among the native troops for want of pay? — Extraction of specie from Bengal for the support of the other Presidencies, the enormous amount of which is stated as the merit of Mr. Hastings? — Investments bought with paper — and draughts on the Directors, and debts accumulating

without

without end ? Put the facts together, and then the House will be able to determine, whether the labour they have at laft undertaken of correcting fo many diforders, and recovering our Indian poffef-feffions from fo many diftreffes, be a tafk of *common* magnitude, or likely to be accomplifhed by *common* men ?

Now, Sir, having difmiffed the ferious part of the honourable gentleman's charge, I hope he will allow me to make a few obfervations on the manner and time, in which it was produced. Suppofing him for a moment to be the reprefentative of Mr. Haftings, and to feel for that gentleman as fenfibly as he could do for himfelf, I beg leave to obferve to him, that his feverity to me is not juftified on any principle of retaliation. I never fought for Mr. Haftings's letters. The honourable gentleman himfelf brought them before the Houfe, and triumphantly referred the contents of them to an attentive examination. But, if it had been otherwife, I cannot admit, that an inoffenfive pleafantry, which wounds no man, and fometimes enlivens the gravity of debate, is equitably retorted by a ferious deliberate attack upon the moral conduct or character of an opponent. It is not likely that I fhould ever have occafion to make a fimilar reflection on that of the honourable gentleman. His actions are too well guarded, and my difpofition to him is too amicable, to allow me to fuppofe the probability of fuch a cafe. Admitting it neverthelefs to happen, I certainly fhould not follow the example he has fet me.
I would

I would not endeavour to take him by furprife. I fhould not expect him to carry letters or tranfactions of ten years ftanding, correctly in his memory. If I thought myfelf obliged to bring a charge of any kind againft him, I fhould think myfelf much more bound, in honour and in juftice, to give him previous notice of my intention, and warn him to prepare for his defence.

I am now to reply to the learned gentleman oppofite to me, and with that I fhall conclude. A challenge from him undoubtedly does me honour, for it fuppofes, in *his* mind at leaft, an idea, which does not exift in mine, and could not have occurred to any other, that, on the fubject in queftion, there is fome approach to equality from me to him. Not being converfant in the forms of the Houfe, I did not know, until fome fome hours later in the fame evening, that I was at liberty to write down the words of gentlemen, uttered perhaps haftily in debate*, for the purpofe of anfwering them at a future occafion. — In a day or two after, I endeavoured to recollect the learned gentleman's words, and I believe I have taken them very exactly. If not, I hope he will do me the favour to correct them. He faid, " That gentlemen had talked in a loofe " general way of difobedience of orders, without " coming to particulars; — that if they would point " out inftances, he fhould know where to *grapple*

---

* Mr. Dundas had quoted words of Mr. Fox, which he faid he had taken down two years ago.

K   " with

" with them. — With refpect to the Maratta war,
" he affirmed that Mr. Haftings was not guilty of
" difobedience of orders; — that the Directors
" themfelves were to blame, in forming and en-
" couraging a plan of conqueft on the Malabar
" coaft, and that Mr. Haftings, in commencing
" and purfuing the Maratta war, had not difobey-
" ed orders, but had conformed to the views of
" the Directors. — That Mr. Haftings neverthelefs
" was greatly to blame for violating the treaty of
" Poorunder. On the truth of thefe affertions,
" the learned gentleman challenged me, and de-
" clared himfelf ready to meet me at any time and
" on any ground *."

I muft confefs, Sir, that this language, efpecial-
ly from the learned gentleman, appeared to me
very extraordinary. I hardly ever heard any thing
with greater furprife. He has employed himfelf,
near two years together, with infinite induftry and
toil, in an inquiry into the abufes that prevail in the
India Company's fervice. — He has publifhed the
refult of his laborious inveftigations in many folio
volumes, which, I verily believe, no man in the
kingdom has read but myfelf. — The prefent bill,
of which the learned gentleman is *prochein ami†*, if
not parent, fuppofes *wilful difobedience* in every department of the fervice; — the conftant complaint

* Mr. Dundas affented to the exactnefs of this recital of his words.

† A term ufed in law for him, who is the next friend, or next
of kin to a child in his nonage.

of

of the Directors has been that their orders are not obeyed; and finally the right honourable gentleman, who propofes the bill, particularly urged and infifted on the neceffity of conquering a fpirit of refiftance, univerfally prevailing among the Company's fervants in India. On any other prefumption, the claufe would be fuperfluous. In the face of all this evidence and authority, the learned gentleman gravely affures the Houfe, that there have been no examples of difobedience, or that the inftances, if any, have not been material. He calls upon his opponents to come to particulars, and then he fhall know where to *grapple* with them. Sir, I will not weary the Houfe with a multitude of quotations from the Company's records. They are filled with the very proofs and examples, which the learned gentleman calls for. Setting afide orders indifferent to the fervants abroad, and which of courfe they had no motive to difobey, and fetting afide orders, which were capable of being converted to fome purpofe of their own, — for thefe they have obeyed not only with exactnefs but oftentation, I affirm that, fo far from its being difficult to find inftances of difobedience, the difficulty would be to point out an order of the Directors, that ever was regarded. The India Company little know, in what fort of eftimation their Directors are held in India. But it is proper I fhould encounter the learned gentleman on his own ground. Let him afk the Directors, what they think of the following examples. They are not mere facts, for which excufes or pre-

tences

tences might be invented, but formal acts of diso-
bedience, deliberately avowed and defended on
principle.

The first is the well-known case of Mr. John
Briftow, who had been recalled by Mr. Haftings
from his ftation at Lucknow, without any charge
whatever againft his conduct, and whom the Directors repeatedly ordered to be re-inftated. Your Select Committee * have reported to you, in what
manner thofe orders were regarded. The general
ground taken and avowed by Mr. Haftings was, that
the orders in queftion invaded *his prerogative*, and
he fhould be degraded by obeying them.

The fecond is the cafe of Mr. Francis Fowke,
which has alfo been fully reported to you by your
Select Committee. This gentleman was recalled
from Benares by Mr. Haftings, who declared
that there was *no charge nor the flighteft imputation
of a charge againft him*. The Directors repeatedly
ordered him to be re-inftated, but to no purpofe. In
their letter of the 27th of May, 1779, they fay,
" We have read, with aftonifhment, your *formal*
" refolution, to fufpend the execution of our orders
" relative to Mr. Francis Fowke; your proceed-
" ings at large are now before us; we fhall take
" fuch meafures as appear neceffary for preferving
" the authority of the Court of Directors, and for
" preventing fuch inftances of *direct and wilful dif-*
" *obedience* in our fervants in time to come." On

* Ninth Report, page 56.

this

this occasion, the principle maintained by Mr. Barwell was, that " he muft decline an acquiefcence " in *any* order, which had *a tendency* to bring the " Government into difrepute."

If the learned gentleman fays, that thefe are inftances of no great moment, I fhall leave him to fettle that queftion with the Directors. Inftead of combating his opinion, I fhall take the liberty of afking him, whether he ferioufly means to refer it to the Company's fervants to determine, whether the orders they receive are material or not. If he does, I can venture to affure him, that the latitude he allows is fufficient to anfwer all their purpofes, and that they are not fo unreafonable, as to defire any greater.

The bufinefs of contracts alone has opened a wide and fertile field of difobedience. The fundamental principle laid down by the Company was, that all contracts fhould be annual ; that the Government fhould advertife for propofals, and always give a preference to the loweft bidders. Thefe rules, I prefume, would be deemed unexceptionable, if they did not limit the patronage of men in power in India, or the profits of their friends. Mr. Haftings and Mr. Barwell gave all the contracts, to perfons of their own choice, on their own terms, for five years inftead of one, and without advertifing for propofals. I beg the learned gentleman will attend to what the Directors themfelves have faid upon the fubject. In their letter of the 23d of December, 1778, among many other obfervations, they fay,

Par.

Par. 59. " This *waſte of our property* cannot be
" permitted. You † have diſregarded our autho-
" rity, and diſobeyed our orders, in not taking the
" loweſt offers."

77. " In order to prevent the Company's money
" from being thus *given away in future,* we poſi-
" tively direct," &c. &c.

99. " With theſe materials before you, the queſ-
" tion is put, whether the contractor's terms, or
" the propoſals of Mr. Johnſon, ſhall be accepted :
" Mr. Francis, in ſtrict conformity with the Com-
" pany's orders, and according to eſtabliſhed uſage,
" was of opinion, that the contract ſhould be ad-
" vertiſed. Mr. Barwell thought the preſent con-
" tractor had, the preceding year, by making low
" propoſals (to uſe his own phraſe) ejected Mr.
" Johnſon, in hopes of obtaining future indulgence,
" and therefore he could not heſitate to give his
" vote for Mr. Johnſon."

100. " However ſtrange Mr. Barwell's motive,
" for giving his vote for Mr. Johnſon, may appear
" to us, we muſt confeſs, the Governor General's
" reaſons for concurring therein were ſtill more
" extraordinary. His words are, *I diſapprove of*
" *publiſhing for propoſals ; this contract is reduced too*
" *low already, and will require a vigilant attention to*
" *it on the part of the commanding officer of the corps*
" *of the army, that it will be duly performed ;* to
" which he adds, *that according to the beſt informa-*

† Mr. Haſtings and Mr. Barwell.

" *tion*

" tion he had been able to obtain, little profit would
" be made by the contractor, if he did his duty."

101. " But although the Governor General has
" thought proper to exprefs fo direct and pointed a
" difapprobation of the mode adopted and pofitive-
" ly enjoined by the Company, for conducting fo
" great a branch of their affairs, as that of the army
" contract, we neverthelefs adhere to the propriety
" of the Court's orders," &c.

If this part of the fubject fhould be thought to
require any farther proof or explanation, the Records of the India Houfe will furnifh it in abundance. If the learned gentleman be ftill diffatisfied,
if he ftill has any paffion for combat, I fhall leave
him to *grapple* with the Court of Directors.

I do not perfectly underftand the learned gentleman, when he fays, in the fame breath, that Mr.
Haftings is not anfwerable for the fecond Maratta
war, *though he was greatly to blame for violating the
treaty of Poorundur.* The breach of the treaty and
the war are one and the fame act. When he broke
the treaty, he created the war. But it feems, he
did it in compliance with inftructions from the
Court of Directors. Had that been the fact, it
would have redounded to the credit of Mr. Haftings, if, in that inftance, he had treated their orders with the fame difregard, which he did in every
other. He would then have had the real merit of
fupporting the permanent fundamental principles,
the wife pacific policy of the India Company againft
an incidental order from a fluctuating Direction.

But

But it is not fo. Sir, I am not a profeffed advocate of the Court of Directors, and they are very well able to defend themfelves. In this inftance, however, it is but juftice to them to fay, that they have not been juftly accufed. Firft of all, let us confider what the Company's acknowledged fyftem is. If I am not very ill informed, the learned gentleman himfelf has heretofore declared, that their *written* inftructions would compofe a perfect code of political wifdom.

In the very firft article of their general inftructions to Bengal, dated the 29th of March, 1774, they fay, " We direct, that you fix your attention " to the prefervation of peace throughout India, " and to the *fecurity* of the poffeffions and revenues " of the Company."

In their letter of the 15th of December, 1775, they fay,

Par. 4. " We difapprove all fuch diftant ex-" peditions, as may eventually carry our forces to " any fituation, too remote to admit of their fafe " and fpeedy return to the protection of our pro-" vinces, in cafes of emergency."

5. " We alfo *utterly* difapprove and condemn of-" fenfive wars; diftinguifhing, however, between " offenfive meafures unneceffarily undertaken with " a view to pecuniary advantages, and thofe, which " the prefervation of our honour, or the protection " or fafety of our poffeffions, may render abfolutely " neceffary."

6. " The

6. " The attention paid by the *majority* * to the
" tenor and fpirit of our orders on this fubject, is
" highly agreeable to us ; and it is our moft pofi-
" tive direction, that no deviation from thofe or-
" ders be permitted, but upon the moft urgent and
" abfolute neceffity ; as that alone can juftify a de-
" parture from them ; for the profpect of any ad-
" vantages, however alluring, can in no wife be
" adequate to the pernicious confequences which
" muft refult from examples of difobedience to our
" orders."

7. " The fentiments expreffed by the *majority* †,
" in the thirty-fixth paragraph of their addrefs,
" coincide exactly with our own ; their determina-
" tion to endeavour to maintain peace in India, and
" vigoroufly to defend our poffeffions and allies,
" cannot be too much applauded : we therefore
" ftrictly enjoin every member of our Council, to
" concur heartily in fuch meafures as may be ne-
" ceffary for accomplifhing thefe defirable pur-
" pofes."

8. " We have already, in our letter of the 3d of
", March, 1775, expreffed our extreme concern, in
" finding that our arms had been employed in con-
" quering the Rohilla country for Sujah Dowlah,
" and difapproved the meafure ; and we have no
" reafon to alter our fentiments refpecting that
" tranfaction."

* Clavering, Monfon, and Francis.
† Ditto.

In

In their general inſtructions to the Commiſſioners appointed in the year 1769, they ſay, " In all your " treaties with the country powers you are to take " care, that they be ſo framed, as neither imme- " diately nor eventually to engage the Company in " any diſputes between thoſe powers."

Theſe documents, out of a multitude, are ſuffi-' cient to eſtabliſh the general views and principles of the Court of Directors. With reſpect to the par- ticular point in queſtion, it happens that they gave a particular injunction. In a letter of the 4th of July, 1777, they ſay, " Though the treaty (of " Poorundur) is not, on the whole, ſo agreeable to " us, as we could wiſh, ſtill we are reſolved ſtrict- " ly to adhere to it on our parts." If the Direc- tors could have been mad enough to ſend out or- ders to ſet aſide thoſe, which I have recited to the Houſe, deprivation of power would be but a ſmall portion of the puniſhment their conduct would de- ſerve.

A word or two of perſonal application to the learned gentleman, and I have done. I have ob- ſerved with concern, that his mind is not ſo perfect- ly free, as it ought to be, from uneaſy ſenſations. He is conſcious that, amidſt contending parties, he has done his duty impartially ; — that, in ſpeaking of Mr. Haſtings, his language had been exactly ba- lanced between condemnation and applauſe ; — that he never ſaid that Mr. Haſtings was either a very good man or a very bad man ; meaning, as we all do, the political principles of the governor, not the

moral

moral character of the man; and that having pur-
fued this middle, even courfe, without the fmalleft
inclination to either fide, he had not had the good
fortune to fatisfy any body. This indeed is too
often the lot of moderate men in violent times. But
I have great pleafure in being able to affure the
learned gentleman, that *his* lot is directly the reverfe of what he thinks it: Inftead of pleafing no-
body, he has had the wifdom to obferve a conduct,
by which every individual of every party has been
gratified in his turn. I fhall contribute to the public fervice, if I can affift in relieving him from this
ill-founded apprehenfion. He cannot be difturbed
in his application to bufinefs, without injury to the
public. To remove one half of his apprehenfions
I need only read to him fome of his own refolutions
regarding Mr. Haftings, which I dare fay he has
totally forgotten.

" *Extracts from the Refolutions of the Committee of*
 " *Secrecy,* 28th *May,* 1782.

Refolved, 18. " That the refolution of the ma-
 " jority of the Supreme Council, on the 2d of
 " February, 1778, which, by the death of Colo-
 " nel Monfon, was now decided by the cafting
 " voice of the Governor General, had a ftrong ten-
 " dency to a renewal of the Maratta war."
   35. " That the inftructions and powers given
 " to Colonel Goddard by the Supreme Council, on

" the 5th of April, 1779, fixed on them, from that
" time, the chief direction and refponfibility of
" the war with the Marattas."

39. " That it muft be reckoned among the many,
" additional mifchiefs, which have arifen chiefly
" from this improvident war with the Marattas to
" the Company's affairs, that the military force of
" the Carnatic had been weakened by reinforce-
" ments fent to the Malabar coaft ; — that the
" Bengal Government have been under the ne-
" ceffity of fupporting on their confines the army
" of a power, confederated, however involuntarily,
" againft them ; that they have been obliged to fue
" for the mediation of the fame power, *(the Rajah*
" *of Berar)* have fubmitted to a refufal, and pur-
" chafed at leaft an uncertain, becaufe apparently
" an unauthorifed treaty, *on moft extravagant and*
" *difhonourable conditions*, with his fon, Rajah Chim-
" najee ; and finally, that, being burthened with
" the expences of a variety of diftant expeditions,
" while their allies are in diftrefs, and their tribu-
" taries under oppreffion, there is alfo an alarming
" deficiency in their own refources of revenue and
" commerce, by the accumulation of their debt,
" and the reduction of their inveftment."

40. " That the attempt made by the Govern-
" ment General in the month of January, 1781,
" to form an engagement of alliance, offenfive and
" defenfive, with the Dutch Eaft-India Company,
" by the means, and upon the terms ftated in the
                                        " proceedings

" proceedings of their Council, was *unwarranted,*
" *impolitic, extravagant, and unjuft.*"

42. " That the Government of Bengal had been
" previoufly in poffeffion of a letter from the Duan
" of the Rajah of Berar, containing overtures for
" mediation for peace and alliance with the *Pefhwa* ;
" and that this material information was wholly
" fuppreffed by them in their difpatches to the
" Court of Directors, but a copy of it was fent
" by the fame conveyance *to the private agent of*
" *Mr. Haftings* ; and that, in thus neglecting to
" make immediate communication to the Court of
" Directors of fuch important intelligence, the Go-
" vernment General appear to have failed in an
" effential part of their duty."

Refolved, " That Warren Haftings, Efq. Go-
" vernor General in Bengal, and William Hornby,
" Efq. Prefident of the Council at Bombay, have-
" ing, in fundry inftances, acted in a manner *re-*
" *pugnant to the honour and policy of this nation, and*
" *thereby brought great calamities on India, and enor-*
" *mous expences on the Eaft-India Company,* it is the
" duty of the Directors of the faid Company to
" purfue all legal and effectual means for the re-
" moval of the faid Governor General and Prefi-
" dent from their faid offices, and to recal them to
" Great Britain."

This, Sir, I conceive, is not the language of a
man very much undecided in his opinion, or who
hefitates between the extremes of cenfure and approbation.

probation. If it be, I fhould be glad to know, in what terms the learned gentleman would exprefs himfelf, when he ferioufly intended to condemn. I can truly affure him that I am not acquainted with any man, fo hoftile to Mr. Haftings, as not to be contented with this defcription of his conduct. So peremptory and decided is the condemnation ex-preffed in thefe Refolutions, that feveral of my friends in India concluded they had been drawn up by *me*. Knowing nothing of the ftate of men and things in this country, they drew their conclufion from the knowledge they had of my opinions, and from that very character of decifion, which is ftamped on the face of the Refolutions, and which the learned gentleman thinks it prudent to difclaim. The fondnefs and applaufe, with which he has lately fpoken of Mr. Haftings, have compleatly reconciled him to that gentleman's friends. All parties now have been fatisfied in fucceffion; and in this fenfe, I confefs the learned gentleman has been impartial. His cenfure and applaufe are diftributed with an equal hand, and fo the account is balanced.

. I told my Indian friends, in return to their let-ters, that I indeed had no concern in the matter; but that the bufinefs was happily undertaken by a man of great induftry, of eminent ability, and un-exampled perfeverance, who, I was fure, would carry it through. Of his induftry and ability, my opinion is the fame;—but I am forced to acknow-ledge, that perfeverance, fuch as his, is not without example.

example. — Other men are obliged to employ their talents in one line, and direct their efforts to one object; and, even with this limitation, it is well if they fucceed. — The learned gentleman's abilities are not fo narrowly confined. He carries the application of them to every extreme, and equally fucceeds in exerting them in every direction.

APPEN.

A P P E N D I X.

No. I.

IN the courfe of the debate on the 16th of July, it was infifted by a learned gentleman, in defence of the new Judicature, that the erection of fome new tribunal was neceffary, for that Juries would be found unequal to the tafk of trying mifdemeanors committed in India. In fupport of this pofition, he contended that the trials of offences within the purview of this bill would probably be of great length; that many might laft more than a week; and that fome might laft even more than a month. He then proceeded to obferve, that common Jurymen were not *fit* to have fuch caufes brought before them. With regard to the probable length of the trials, it is fcarcely poffible that trials fhould be fpun out to fuch a length, as he feemed to apprehend, even in this new Court, though in fome refpects it feems calculated for the purpofes of delay. When any teftimony is to be brought from India, a mandamus muft iffue from the King's Bench, and the depositions,

positions, taken by virtue of it, must be tranfmitted to England, before even the commiffion can
iffue from the Court of Chancery for holding the
Court. All the teftimony, that is to come from
abroad, muft be collected, even before the Court
is in exiftence. What reafon then is there to fear
that, when the foreign evidence is to be thus prepared, trials would in general be of long conti-
nuance ? If they fhould, it would be owing, not to
difficulties in the procuring or examination of evidence, but to the power given to the Commiffioners
to adjourn from time to time, as they fhall think fit ;
a power which would indeed, in all probability, be
productive of the greateft delays in the adminiftration of juftice. But it may be afked, why a Jury is
not as competent to try a mifdemeanor committed in
India, as one committed in England; and why a
greater time fhould be neceffary for the trial of the
former than of the latter ? The affirmative refts on
an affertion, which, ftanding without argument,
need only be denied. No man can be tried, even
under the provifions of this bill, on an accumulated
or general charge. The information or indictment
muft be for fome fpecific offence or offences, to
which the party is to plead, and upon which iffue
muft be joined. If there be any teftimony in India,
it is to be tranfmitted under a mandamus to England.
After all this preparation then, (a preparation which
is prefcribed by the bill) a mifdemeanor committed
in India may be tried by a Jury with as little difficulty, and in as little time, as one committed in

M   England.

England. The learned gentleman's doctrine is of the most dangerous tendency : it leads to the abolition of trial by Jury. All the arguments, which have been used to shew the inconvenience and impropriety of this mode of trial in cases of offences committed abroad, might with equal force be urged against the propriety of it in cases of offences committed in England ; and very probably we shall soon have them introduced for that purpose.

Let it be admitted, for the sake of argument, that the investigation of Indian misdemeanors will probably take up a long time, and that common Juries are not *fit* to have such causes brought before them ; — still it does not follow that there is any necessity for abolishing trial by Jury. All Indian misdemeanors might be tried by special Juries, and this would obviate the fastidious objection, on which so much stress has been laid. Special Juries are not " chosen out of the mass of mankind," but out of the principal freeholders of the county. Men as little subject to bias, " as little likely to go into " common ale-houses, and enter into porter-club " conversations upon the evidence before them," and as little liable to be misled, as the members of either House of Parliament.

As for the length of the trials, let the investigation be ever so long, a Jury is competent to it. With deference to learned authority, there is no reason to admit that " his going into his box, and " remaining there locked up till he has given his " verdict, is an essential characteristic of a Jury-
" man,

" man."—It is effential that, after the Jury leave
the bar, they fhall not fpeak with the parties or
their agents; and that they fhall receive no frefh
evidence: and it is common, in order to prevent
intemperance, or caufelefs delay, to keep them
without meat, drink, fire, or candle; but I affirm
that this is not effential: the law fays, that, by
permiffion of the Judge, they may be allowed fire,
candle, and refrefhments. That permiffion would
always be given, when the length and nature of the
teftimony might render much deliberation neceffary,
and thus the Jury would have it in their power,
without any material inconvenience to themfelves,
to give full confideration to every part of the bufinefs before them.

No. II.

*Minute of Richard Barwell, Efq. recorded in Conful-
tation of 7th of November, 1774, and referred to
in Page 27.*

" I entirely approve of the Honourable the Pre-
" fident's conduct in the *receipt* of complimentary
" nuzzers.

" The prejudices of the natives of Hindoftan,
" bigoted to their ancient cuftoms, make it *abfo-
" lutely impoffible* to avoid deviating in this particu-
" lar from the words of the Act of Parliament!
" The fpirit of the act is not, however, by this

" feeming

" feeming deviation, departed from, but regarded
" with an attention, *which shews the most scrupulous*
" *respect to the restrictions of the Legislature!* Nuz-
" zers are not made to the man, but to the station
" he fills, and are very different in their nature
" from *gratuitous rewards*, or the gifts, denomi-
" nated presents ; I therefore cannot but equally
" honour the principle, while I admire the justness
" of the motive, on which official nuzzers, or
" compliments are *accepted* by the Governor Gene-
" ral.   I fee their *acceptance* in a light of the
" greatest propriety, perfectly consistent with the
" ideas of the Company, and regardful of what
" they have invariably recommended, attention to
" the particular prejudices, manners, and disposi-
" tions of the natives !

" The Governor General has thought proper to
" submit the nuzzers, made to *his* station, to the
" Court of Directors, to be appropriated agree-
" ably to their pleasure.   Small as the object is to
" the Company and to the nation, it gives dignity
" to *his* character as guardian of the public inte-
" rests, and obviates all misrepresentation of the
" principle and the motive, which has induced
" him to a compliance with the rooted prejudices
" and manners of the Asiatics.   *My* experience,
" from a long residence in this country, convinces
" me of the *real necessity* there is of respecting
" usages *in immaterial points*, and which, disre-
" garded, would be followed by impressions re-
" sulting from a conduct repugnant to Asiatic
" notions

" notions of propriety and deference. I might
" here make a tender to the Public of the trivial
" nuzzers, to the acceptance of which my ſtation
" has *impelled* me ; but what is proper in the Go-
" vernor General, would in me, I apprehend, ap-
" pear *rather in the light of a conſequential inſignifi-*
" *cant diſplay of rigidneſs in exceſs ! !* The amount
" of my complimentary nuzzers of a gold mohur,
" and five rupees, from the period of my arrival at
" the Preſidency; exceeds not the ſum of two hun-
" dred and fifty rupees, excluſive of a compliment
" from the Nabob of Arcot of a few pieces of
" cloth, the produce of his country, and two
" ſhauls, a compliment more than returned by
" myſelf in the manufactures of Bengal, to the
" amount of three thouſand Sicca rupees.

(Signed)   " RICHARD BARWELL."

No. III.

*Extract of the General Inſtructions, given by the Court
of Directors to the Governor General and Council of
Fort William, dated the 29th of March, 1774, and
confirmed by a General Court of Proprietors.*

35. " W E direct, that you immediately cauſe
" the ſtricteſt inquiry to be made into all op-
" preſſions, which may have been committed, ei-
" ther againſt the natives or Europeans, and into
" all

" all abuſes that may have prevailed in the collec-
" tion of the revenues, or any part of the civil go-
" vernment of the Preſidency ; and that you com-
" municate to us all information, which you may
" be able to obtain relative thereto, or to any diſſi-
" pation or embezzlement of the Company's mo-
" ney."

*Extract of a General Letter from the Court of Direc-
tors to the Governor General and Council, dated the
5th of April,* 1776.

Par. 27. " HAVING inveſtigated the charges
" exhibited againſt ſome of the members of our
" late Adminiſtration, we have come to the follow-
" ing reſolutions :
Reſolved, " That it appears that the conduct of
" the late Preſident* and Council of Fort William
" in Bengal, in ſuffering *Cantoo-Baboo,* the preſent
" Governor General's Banyan, to hold farms in dif-
" ferent Purgunnahs to a large amount, or to be
" ſecurity for ſuch farms, contrary to the tenor and
" ſpirit of the ſeventeenth regulation of the Com-
" mittee of Revenue at Fort William, of the 14th
" of May, 1772, and afterwards relinquiſhing that
" ſecurity without ſatisfaction made to the Com-
" pany, was highly improper, and has been at-
" tended with conſiderable loſs to the Company.

* Mr. Haſtings.

Reſolved,

Refolved, " That it appears that a confiderable
" fum of money has been given by one of the
" Company's tenants, for holding the falt farms of
" Selimabad and Duccann-Savagepore, in the dif-
" trict of Dacca, over and above the engagement
" for thofe farms to the Company, contrary to the
" letter and fpirit of the eleventh regulation of the
" Committee of Revenue, of the 14th of May,
" 1772 ; and that Mr. *Barwell* has acknowledged
" having charged the faid tenant, for his own ufe,
" and the other gentlemen of the Factory, with
" the amount of 125,500 rupees, for permitting
" him to hold the faid farms."

28. " Since paffing the above refolutions, the
" Northumberland's Purfer is arrived with your
" advices ; and our concern is much increafed on
" finding that improper influence, and interference
" of our fervants in the revenue branch, has been
" much more general than we had been led to hope
" was the cafe ; and that in the immediate views of
" private gain, the Company's intereft has been
" greatly neglected."

30. " The powers and inftructions vefted in, and
" given to General Clavering and the other gentle-
" men, were fuch as fully authorifed them in every
" inquiry that feems to have been their object ;
" *and we highly commend the indefatigable affiduity*
" *that evidently appears in their laborious refearches,*
" *and their zeal for the intereft of the Company and the*
" *welfare of individuals, as well natives as Euro-*
" *peans.*"

Extract

Extract of a General Letter from the Court of Direc-
tors to the Governor General and Council, dated the
28th of November, 1777.

39. " WE find that the farm of *Sylhet* was
" granted by the Committee of Circuit; that the
" Company's advances to the farmers of *Sylhet*, of
" 33,000 rupees for elephants, *was received by one*
" *of the members of that Committee.* It has, how-
" ever, since appeared, that the other ostensible
" farmers, or persons named in the Committee's
" settlement, NEVER EXISTED; and that the
" Company's Resident at *Sylhet*, was the real far-
" mer, *under fictitious names.*"

No. IV.

The thirty-third clause of the original bill,
which Mr. Francis desired might be translated into
common sense, is omitted in the amended bill. No
skill in language could translate it. — Vide page 13.

No. V.

The eighteenth resolution of the Committee of
Secrecy, of which Mr. Dundas, then Lord Advocate of Scotland, was Chairman, is guilty of an
anachronism, in which the assertion of a false fact

is

is involved. It afferts that, " in February, 1778, " the refolution of the majority of the Supreme " Council, *by the death of Colonel Monfon*, was now " decided by the cafting voice of the Governor " General." — It was not the death of Colonel Monfon, which gave Mr. Haftings the cafting voice in February, 1778. He died about the end of September, 1776. It was the death of Sir John Clavering, in Auguft, 1777, which gave Mr. Haf- tings a majority at the period in queftion. If the General had been alive in February, 1778, he, Mr. Francis, and Mr. Wheler, would have formed a majority againft Mr. Haftings and Mr. Barwell, and prevented the Maratta war. The refolution, by *fuppofing* General Clavering to be alive, transfers to *him*, becaufe he is dead, the merit of the refiftance, made in Council to that meafure, and keeps the ef- forts of Mr. Francis to prevent a rupture with the Marattas, compleatly out of fight.

THE END.